PROCEEDINGS

OF THE

National Convention

TO SECURE THE

RELIGIOUS AMENDMENT

OF THE

CONSTITUTION OF THE UNITED STATES.

HELD IN NEW YORK, FEB. 26 AND 27, 1873.

With an Account of the Origin and Progress of the Movement.

NEW YORK:
JOHN POLHEMUS, PRINTER, 102 NASSAU ST.
1873.

CONTENTS.

HISTORY OF THE MOVEMENT
TO SECURE THE RELIGIOUS AMENDMENT
OF THE
CONSTITUTION OF THE UNITED STATES.

BY T. P. STEVENSON,
Corresponding Secretary of the National Association.

The reader of the arguments presented in the following pages will naturally desire some information concerning the history of the movement, the auspices under which it arose, and the methods by which it has been prosecuted during the ten years of its history.

The religious defect of the Constitution of the United States was not unnoticed at the beginning. Luther Martin, a delegate from Maryland to the Convention which framed it, said: "There were some of the members so unfashionable as to think that a belief of the existence of a Deity, and of a future state of rewards and punishments, would be some security for the good conduct of our rulers, and that in a Christian country it would be at least decent to hold some distinction between the professors of Christianity and downright infidelity and paganism."*

On the 28th of October, 1789, the First Presbytery Eastward in Massachusetts and New Hampshire presented a loyal and patriotic address to President Washington, in which, after expressing their satisfaction in beholding how easily the entire confidence of the people in the man first entrusted with the administration of the new Constitution had eradicated every remaining objection to its form, they add: "Among these [objections] we never considered the want of a religious test—that grand engine of persecution in every tyrant's hand—but we should not have been alone in rejoicing to have seen some explicit acknowledgment of the only true God and Jesus Christ, whom He hath sent, inserted somewhere in the Magna Charta of our country."

In the early part of the present century the eminent Dr. John M. Mason, of New York, employed these words: "One would imagine that no occasion of making a pointed and public acknowledgment of the Divine benignity could have presented itself so obviously as the framing an instrument of government which, in the nature of things, must be closely allied to our happiness or our ruin; and yet that very Constitution, which the singular goodness of God enabled us to establish, does not so much as recognize His being."

---

* Genuine Information delivered to the Legislature of Maryland, by Luther Martin, a Delegate. Philadelphia, 1788, page 80.

In the admirable treatise on "The Oath," by the Rev. D. X. Junkin, D. D., published in 1845, the writer says: "The oath of the President of the United States could as well be taken by a pagan or a Mohammedan as by the Chief Magistrate of a Christian people: it excludes the name of the Supreme Being. Indeed, it is negatively *atheistical*, for no God is appealed to at all. In framing many of our public formularies, greater care seems to have been taken to adapt them to the prejudices of the infidel few than to the consciences of the Christian millions. In these things the minority in our country has hitherto managed to govern the majority. * * We look on the designed omission of it [the name of God in the oath] as an attempt to exclude from civil affairs Him who is the Governor among the nations."

These views have been intelligently and firmly maintained by a portion of the American people at all times since the adoption of the present Constitution. The contrast in this respect between the Constitution of the nation and the Constitutions of nearly all the States did not escape observation, and it was remembered that, before the national Constitution, no similar instrument of government had been framed by any portion of the American people without an explicit acknowledgment of Almighty God and the Christian religion.

No public effort to remedy this defect was possible, however, while the question of slavery was agitating the public mind. The intense feeling engendered by that controversy, and the sensitiveness to any proposal to change the Constitution, precluded even the consideration of the subject. With the war, however, there came a change. That great calamity was almost universally felt to be an expression of the Divine displeasure against the nation. The public conscience was prepared to welcome any measure which proposed in a suitable and becoming way to give honor to the God whom we had offended, and express our feelings of repentance and our purpose of reformation. The feelings of a large part of the nation were expressed in the following sentences from a sermon by the Rev. Henry A. Boardman, of Philadelphia, in the year 1862: "We must 'search and try our ways, and turn again to the Lord.' The loss of His favor will explain everything that has happened. And the grand aim should be to learn how we have lost His favor, and by what means we can regain it. This is too large a theme to be discussed within the compass of a few pages, but there is one feature of our Government too closely connected with this question, and too conspicuous, to be passed by in silence. I refer, as you will readily suppose—for the topic is a familiar one—to the absence of any adequate recognition of the sovereignty of God and the religion of which He is the author and object, in our Constitution, and in the practical administration of our political system. * * * Our national charter pays no homage to the Deity. His name does not once occur in the Constitution of the United States. And as if to confound the charity which would refer this omission to some accidental agency, the same atheism is repeated and perpetuated in another form no less inexcusable. The coinage of money is one of the inalienable prerogatives of political sovereignty. The solemnity attached to the function has been recognized by most nations, ancient and modern, Jewish and Christian, Mohammedan and Pagan. You have but to look at the money of any people to know at what altars they worshipped. But *the coinage of the United States is without a God.* * * * Has not the time come to make our formal national confession of this fundamental truth—to impress it on our coinage, to insert it (peradventure it may not be too late) as the keystone of our riven and tottering Constitution."

A Convention for prayer and Christian conference with special reference to the state of the country, had been called to meet at Xenia, Ohio, on the 3d day of February, 1863. When it assembled, it was found to include representatives from eleven different denominations of Christians, and from seven of the States of the Union. An unusual degree of patriotic and religious fervor pervaded all its exercises. It was therefore an auspicious hour for the consideration of the subject when on the second day of its sessions, Mr. John Alexander, then of Xenia, now of Philadelphia, quietly laid on the table of the Convention a paper calling attention to this defect, and proposing that the Convention should take such steps as might seem proper toward its correction. With a view to bring the subject more definitely before the Convention, a form of amendment to the Preamble of the Constitution was suggested, which embodied all the principles which have been advocated in the course of the movement, and which has not since been materially changed.

Notwithstanding some objections that were offered, the paper was received with great unanimity, and referred to a Committee representing all denominations of Christians gathered in the Convention, and the report of this Committee, approving the spirit and design of the paper, and endorsing the action which it proposed, was adopted. From these facts it will be seen that the present movement is the fruit of intelligent and mature conviction, confirmed by long reflection and careful study of the spirit and history of our institutions, and quickened into active effort in an hour of deep religious and patriotic feeling. The eleven denominations of Christians, represented in the Convention, are witnesses of the unsectarian character of the movement. The devout and prayerful spirit which marked its birth, has never ceased to be among its most noticeable characteristics.

The first National Convention to secure this Amendment was held in Allegheny, on the 27th of January, 1864. It was an earnest, prayerful and encouraging meeting. Its action was as follows:

RESOLUTIONS.

Resolved, 1. That we deem it a matter of paramount interest to the life and prosperity, and permanency of our Nation, that its Constitution be so amended as fully to express the Christian national character.

2. That we are encouraged by the success attending the labors of the friends of this movement to persevere, in the hope that, with the blessing of God, this effort will speedily result in the consummation of this great object.

3. That in the late proclamations of His Excellency, the President of the United States, recommending the observance of days of National fasting, humiliation and prayer, (as suggested by the Senate of the United States,) for the purpose of confessing our National sins, which have provoked the Divine displeasure, and of imploring forgiveness through Jesus Christ—and also days of National thanksgiving for the purpose of making grateful acknowledgment of God's mercies—we have pleasing evidence that God is graciously inclining the hearts of those who are in authority over us, to recognize His hand in the affairs of the Nation, and to cherish a sense of our dependence on Him.

4. That the following Memorial and petition to Congress be circulated throughout the United States for signatures:

MEMORIAL TO CONGRESS.

To the Honorable, the Senate and House of Representatives, in Congress assembled :

We, citizens of the United States, respectfully ask your Honorable bodies to adopt measures for amending the Constitution of the United States, so as to read, in substance, as follows:

"We, the people of the United States, [humbly acknowledging Almighty God as the source of all authority and power in civil government, the Lord Jesus Christ as the Ruler among the nations, and His revealed will as the supreme law of the land, in order to constitute a Christian government] and, in order to form a more perfect union, establish justice, insure domestic tranquillity, provide for the common defense, promote the general welfare, [and secure the inalienable rights and the blessings of life, liberty, and the pursuit of happiness to ourselves, our posterity, and all the people,*] do ordain and establish this Constitution for the United States of America.

"And further: that such changes with respect to the oath of office, slavery, and all other matters, should be introduced into the body of the Constitution, as may be necessary to give effect to these amendments in the preamble. And we, your humble petitioners, will ever pray," etc.

Resolved, That a special Committee be appointed to carry the Memorial to Washington, lay it before the President, and endeavor to get a special message to Congress on the subject, and to lay said Memorial before Congress.

The National Association to secure the Religious Amendment to the Constitution of the United States was organized at this Convention, with JOHN ALEXANDER, Esq., as President; ZADOK STREET, Salem, Ohio (of the Society of Friends), Vice-President; a full list of other officers, and an Executive Committee.

A large delegation was appointed to visit Washington, to urge the proposed Amendment on the attention of President Lincoln. This Committee, embracing Professor J. H. MCILVAINE, D.D., Princeton, N. J.; Professor J. T. PRESSLY, D.D., Penn.; Rev. JOHN DOUGLASS, D.D., Penn.; Rev. D. C. PAGE, D.D., Pa.; Rev. H. H. GEORGE, Ohio; Dr. STERRETT, Pa.; JOHN ALEXANDER, Esq., Ohio; Rev. J. S. T. MILLIGAN, Mich.; Rev. R. A. BROWNE, Pa.; and Rev. A. M. MILLIGAN, Pa., met in Willard's Hotel, Washington, on Tuesday evening, February 9. The Rev. Dr. GURLEY, Rev. Dr. CHANNING, Chaplain of the U. S. Senate, J. J. MARKS, D.D., Rev. B. F. MORRIS, Rev. L. D. JOHNSON, and Rev. N. K. CROWE, of the District of Columbia, met with the delegation, heard the address prepared by Dr. MCILVAINE, the Chairman of the Committee, and gave it their hearty sanction. Most of them signed the address and waited on the President with the delegation. Through the aid of Senator SHERMAN, of Ohio, an arrangement was made with the President for an interview on Wednesday, at 3½ P. M., when the delegation was introduced to the President by Dr. GURLEY, and the Chairman made the following address:

ADDRESS TO THE PRESIDENT.

MR. PRESIDENT:—The object for which we have taken the liberty of trespassing a moment on your precious time, can be explained in very few words. We are the representatives of a mass Convention of Christian people, without distinction of sect or denomination, which was held in Allegheny City, on the 27th and 28th of January last; and we are instructed to lay before your Excellency the action of that Convention.

* This clause was dropped after the Amendment prohibiting Slavery was adopted.

After reading the resolutions of the Convention and the Memorial to Congress, embodying the proposed Amendment, the address continued as follows:

We are encouraged, Mr. President, to hope that you will give the great object for which we pray, your cordial and powerful support, because you have already shown, by many significant acts of your administration, that the principle on which it rests is dear to your heart. This principle is our national responsibility to God, which you have expressly and repeatedly recognized. We remember that when, under one of your predecessors, an anti-Christian power had refused to treat with the United States, on the ground that we were a Christian nation, the objection was removed by the authoritative statement that we, as a nation, had no religion; also, that several of your predecessors refused, when earnestly importuned, to appoint days of national fasting and thanksgiving, for the same reason, whilst you, sir, within the space of a single year, have thrice, by solemn proclamation, called us to either national fasting, humiliation and prayer, for our many and grievous sins, especially our sin of forgetting God, or to national thanksgiving for His unspeakable mercies.

You, moreover, as no other of our Chief Magistrates ever did, have solemnly reminded us of the redeeming grace of our blessed Saviour, and of the authority of the Holy Scriptures over us as a people. By such acts as these, you have awakened a hope in the Christian people of this land, that you represent them in feeling and want of a distinct and plain recognition of the Divine authority in the Constitution of the United States. For we hold it most certain truth, that nations, as such, and not individuals alone, are the subjects of God's moral government, are responsible to Him, and by Him are graciously rewarded for their obedience, or justly punished for their disobedience of His divine laws.

We believe also, that our civil and religious liberties, our free institutions, and all our national prosperity, power and glory, are mercies and blessings derived from God to us through the channel of the Christian religion. Notwithstanding, either from inadvertency, or following some Godless theory of civil government, we have omitted even the mention of His blessed name in the most significant and highest act of the nation.

We believe that in thus leaving God out of our political system, we have grievously sinned against Him, have brought upon ourselves and children His just displeasure, opened the flood-gates of that political corruption which is the mediate, and given occasion to that prodigious development of the spirit of oppression and injury to the negro race, which is the immediate source of our present calamities and sorrows. We believe, therefore, that it is our first duty to repent of this and all our national sins, and to return to our obligations as a Christian people, by acknowledging the true God as our God in our fundamental and organic law, in order that we may consistently implore His merciful interposition in our behalf, to give victory to our national arms, and success to the national cause; to establish the unity of the nation and the authority of the Government, now assaulted and shattered by a horrible rebellion. We ask for no union of Church and State—that is a thing which we utterly repudiate; we ask for nothing inconsistent with the largest religious liberty, or the rights of conscience in any man. We represent no sectarian or denominational object, but one in which all who bear the Christian name, and all who have any regard for the Christian religion, can cordially agree; and one to secure which we are persuaded that any lawful and wise movement would call forth an overwhelming public sentiment in its support.

We, therefore, do earnestly hope that you, our beloved Chief Magistrate, will not be indifferent in our prayer. For, by what you have already done in this cause, and by your integrity, firmness and excellent wisdom, (divinely guided as we believe it has been, and pray that it may ever continue to be,) under the terrible responsibility laid upon you in this, the darkest hour of our country's peril and rebuke, you have won the confidence and affection of the Christian people of this land, beyond all your predecessors, save only the Father of his Country. Knowing, then, the respect and deference with which your sage counsels are listened to by the whole people, and deeming the present time and occasion most opportune, we are persuaded that if you will give this movement your favor and support, it will be successful, and thus you will place yourself in the hearts of the present, and of all future generations, as one of the greatest benefactors of your country. For, having inaugurated those measures which aim to right, so far as that is possible, our great national wrong committed against man, you will have wielded that vast influence with which you have been clothed by Divine Providence and by the voice of the people, to right, so far as that can be done, that great wrong which as a nation we have committed against God, in leaving Him out of our political system.

The President replied as follows :

GENTLEMEN :—The general aspect of your movement, I cordially approve. In regard to particulars, I must ask time to deliberate, as the work of amending the Constitution should not be done hastily. I will carefully examine your paper, in order more fully to comprehend its contents than is possible from merely hearing it read, and will take such action upon it as my responsibility to our Maker and our country demands.

The General Assembly of the Presbyterian Church (O. S.), in session at Newark, in May, 1864, in answer to an overture on the subject from the Synod of the Pacific, adopted the following preamble and resolutions offered by Dr. Musgrave :

Whereas, Almighty God, the God of nations, is the head and source of all authority and power in civil government, and nations as such are the subjects of His moral laws, and His revealed will is the supreme law of national life ;

Whereas, The Christian and loyal people of our country are everywhere beseeching God to interpose for our deliverance as a nation, from the assaults of a most groundless and wicked rebellion, and to establish and maintain the national unity and authority ; and

Whereas, Resolutions have already passed the Senate of the United States, and are pending in the House of Representatives, recommending the Amendment of the National Constitution in several other particulars ; therefore,

Resolved, That it is our solemn national duty so to amend our fundamental and organic law, that the preamble of the National Constitution shall read in substance as follows : "We, the people of the United States," &c., (in the words of the proposed Amendment.)

Resolved, That this General Assembly recommend to all the people in the congregations under its care, to memorialize Congress upon this subject.

As the Allegheny Convention was an intermediate meeting to effect a permanent organization, it was determined to call the First Annual Meeting of the Association in Philadelphia, in July following. It was held accordingly in the Eighth street Methodist Episcopal Church, on Wednesday and Thursday, the 7th and 8th days of that month. Though the meeting was not large, the character and position of those present, and the interest manifested in the cause were exceedingly encouraging. Addresses were made by the Rev. D. C. Eddy, D. D., of the Tabernacle Baptist Church, and the Rev. J. H. A. Bomberger, D. D., of the German Reformed Church. Dr. Eddy was elected President of the Association for the ensuing year. The Revs. T. P. Stevenson and W. W. Spear, D. D., and Wm. Getty, Esq., were appointed a Committee on Correspondence, and were directed to prepare an address to the public in behalf of the cause. From this address, the first issued after the organization of the Asssociation, we extract the following passages:

Many Christians are convinced that we have failed to give our civil institutions that definite and practical religious character which is worthy of a Christian people and essential to national permanence and prosperity. We are not aware that in the formation of our Government, by any act or any declaration, we recognized the divine origin of the institution then set up. While we have distinctly asserted, and jealously maintained, the right of the people to set up forms of government for themselves, we have not acknowledged—it would seem we have not felt—that the constitution of government is an act of obedience to God, and that all legitimate civil authority is ultimately derived from Him. Neither have we recognized the moral responsibility of the nation in its organic character, nor its obligation to accept and obey the will of God revealed in His word. And this defect is made painfully conspicuous by the omission of the name of God even from the form of oath prescribed in the Constitution, which simply reads, "I do solemnly swear or affirm."

THESE AMENDMENTS RIGHT AND NECESSARY.

We respectfully submit to your consideration, whether these amendments are not simply an appropriate recognition of the relations which all just human authority sustains to the Supreme Ruler of the Universe. Is not anything less than this wholly inconsistent with those relations? We propose the recognition of God, not only because He is the Supreme Ruler of all men and al. organizations, but because it is He who has given the institution of civil government to man, and the just authority of the magistrate is derived from Him. "There is no power but of God. The powers that be are ordained of God." It is surely fitting that a constitution framed by a Christian people should recognize a higher source of civil authority than the mere will or consent of the citizen. And in presenting civil government thus, as a divine institution, we enforce, by the highest possible sanctions, its claims upon the respect and obedience of the citizen. The true strength of a government lies in the conscientious regard felt for it as the ordinance of God. Thus only is the magistrate clothed with his true authority, and the majesty of the law suitably preserved. "The sanctions of religion," says De Witt Clinton, "compose the foundations of good government."

The moral character of a government has a powerful reflex influence on the moral character of the people. Especially is this felt in a popular government, where the people are brought into constant contact with it, study its history, admire its provisions, and drink deeply of its spirit. An irreligious government begets an irreligious people. It must be deplored that in a Constitution so universally and so justly admired and loved and studied by the American people, there is nothing to turn the mind of the nation to God, to inculcate reverence for the authority of His Son or respect for His word.

JUSTIFIED BY OUR OWN HISTORY.

The principles which we here present are not new in American politics. We are able to plead many precedents, which must have the weight of authority with the American people. Our country was originally settled by men of high religious character, whose only motive in seeking a home in the wilderness was the freedom and safety of religion, and the glory of God. They left the impress of their character on the civil institutions which they set up. In the cabin of the Mayflower, and before landing on Plymouth Rock, the Pilgrims agreed upon a constitution of civil government, in which they declared "the glory of God and the advancement of the Christian faith" to be among the ends of their organization. This Constitution, beginning: "In the name of God, Amen," invokes, says Webster, "a religious sanction and the authority of God on their civil obligations."

The Constitution of the first government established in the limits of the present State of Connecticut, declares that "where a people are gathered together, the

Word of God requires that there should be an orderly and decent government established according to God."

The first form of government that existed in Pennsylvania asserted "the origination and descent of all human power from God," and the first legislative act of the Colony, passed at Chester in 1662, recognized the Christian religion, while it established liberty of conscience, and declared that the glory of God and the good of mankind are the reason and end of government, which is, therefore, a venerable ordinance of God. And the Supreme Court of Pennsylvania, in 1824, on a trial for blasphemy, referring to this early statute, says: "Christianity—general Christianity—is and always has been a part of the common law of Pennsylvania; not Christianity founded on particular tenets, nor an established Church, with tithes and spiritual courts, but Christianity with liberty of conscience to all men."

The State Constitutions of the era of the Revolution present the same characteristics. In 1780, the Constitution of Massachusetts declared "that the happiness of a people, and the good order and preservation of civil government, essentially depend on piety, religion, and morality." And in the Convention of that State, met in 1820, to revise the Constitution, Mr. Webster said: "I am clearly of opinion that we should not strike out all recognition of the Christian religion. I am desirous that in so solemn a transaction as the establishment of a Constitution we should express our attachment to Christianity—not indeed to any of its peculiar forms, but to its general principles." But it is needless to multiply examples; for of the thirteen States existing originally, not one had failed in its Constitution to make recognition, more or less explicit, of the authority of God and the claims of His law. And it is a matter of deep regret, that when we were enabled, after the triumphant assertion of our independence, to set up a statelier governmental structure, we left out that which constituted the chief strength and glory of those earlier commonwealths.

Whatever explanation we put upon this unfortunate omission, it cannot be considered presumptuous, after the experience of nearly three-quarters of a century, to propose amendments to any constitution, however admirable and beneficent. It has already been amended in some particulars. The present rebellion has led to a general conviction that additional amendments are necessary to secure universal liberty, and prevent even the possible recurrence of the evils which we now suffer. We propose that the Constitution be made unmistakably *Christian*, as well as *free*.

IN ACCORD WITH OUR NATIONAL ACTS.

There are well-established features in our Government, which are consistent only with such principles as we seek to introduce into the National Constitution. Through our whole history chaplains have been appointed by Congress; prayer is offered daily during its sessions, and the nation is called at intervals, by both Congress and the Executive, to thanksgiving, or fasting and prayer. A recent resolution of the Senate on such an occasion, recognized the medium of Jesus Christ, and the President called us to give thanks "for preserving and redeeming grace." We have gone to the Christian religion for the only bond we have for the integrity of the ruler, or the fidelity of the citizen—the divine ordinance of an oath. Such acts can have no meaning, except as a nation we acknowledge God. If such implied recognition of God be proper and becoming, no objection can be urged against the express recognition which we propose. Its necessity will be felt when we remember that one Chief Magistrate once refused to appoint a day of fasting and prayer in an hour of public calamity, because the nation, in its Constitution, recognized no God, and another, in contracting a treaty with a Mohammedan power, hesitated not to declare that "The Government of the United States is not, in any sense, founded on the Christian religion. It has in itself no character of enmity against the laws and religion of Mussulmans."* Surely our Christian character should be so well defined, that the Chief Magistrate of the nation could not doubt or ignore it, so clear that all the world should know us as a nation whose God is Jehovah.

* Treaty with Tripoli. Art. xi. Laws of the United States, vol. 4.

In this movement, prompted by pure Christian patriotism, participated in by various Christian denominations, all of whom are opposed to any sectarian establishment of religion, we invite the co-operation of every lover of his country, and every follower of Jesus Christ. We invite all ministers of the Gospel to proclaim to the nation the claims of Him whose ambassadors they are. We invite the co-operation of all ecclesiastical bodies in this effort to return to our fathers' God, to honor our common Redeemer, and to secure the best interests of our land.

The next Convention was held in the West Arch street Presbyterian Church on the 29th of November, 1864. Ex-Governor Pollock presided, and addresses of unusual interest and power were made by Judge Strong, Dr. Edwards, Dr. McIlvaine, Dr. George Junkin, Dr. Joel Swartz, (Lutheran,) of Baltimore, and the Rev. Dr. Goddard, (Episcopal,) of Philadelphia. Delegates were present from different parts of the country, and altogether it was a very encouraging meeting. The following resolutions were adopted :

Resolved, That a National recognition of God, the Lord Jesus Christ, and the Holy Scriptures, as proposed in the memorial of this Association to Congress, it is clearly a Scriptural duty, which it is National peril to disregard.

Resolved, That, in consideration of the general diffusion of religious intelligence, principles and institutions throughout our country—in view of the many express recognitions of Christianity by the Constitutions and the legislative enactments of the several States—and in view, also, of the religious history of the founders of this Government, it is a striking and solemn fact that our present National Constitution is so devoid of any distinctive Christian feature, that one of our Chief Magistrates once refused to appoint a day of fasting and prayer in an hour of public calamity, because the Nation, in its Constitution, recognized no God; and another, in contracting a treaty with a Mohammedan power, hesitated not to declare that "The Government of the United States is not, in any sense, founded on the Christian religion. It has in itself no character of enmity against the laws and religion of Mussulmans."

Resolved, That the measures proposed by this Association are not sectional, nor sectarian, nor partisan, but the general voice of Christan patriotism, asking that which is right and wholesome, which is in keeping with our antecedents, and which will not operate oppressively upon the conscience of any citizen.

Resolved, That the state of the times, recent and present, and the state of public sentiment, warrants and encourages the attempt to secure the Amendment of the Constitution which is proposed by this Association.

During the subsequent years the movement has been promoted by the holding of annual conventions, the circulation of petitions to Congress, by sermons, public meetings, and addresses before representative bodies, by the distribution of tracts, and by the formation of auxiliary societies. Of these, the National Reform Association of Southern Illinois has had the longest history, and its influence has been most widely felt. Of the conventions, that in New York, in 1866 ; the Ohio State Convention, which met at Columbus, in February, 1869 ; the Northwest Convention, at Monmouth, Illinois, in April, 1871, and the National Convention at Pittsburgh, in 1870, were the most noteworthy. The Pittsburgh Convention gave a marked impulse to the cause. No immediate attempt has been made to secure action by Congress. All the efforts of the Association have been directed to the formation of a right public sentiment on the relation of government to religion,—a sentiment without which the amendment would be as valueless as its adoption would be impossible. For nearly six years the progress of the movement, and the labors in its behalf, have been faithfully chronicled in the pages of the CHRISTIAN STATESMAN, a paper established by the writer of this sketch, and the Rev. D. McAllister, for the advocacy of this cause. Established at first as the individual contribution of its editors to the cause, and issued only semi-monthly, it has lately been enlarged and is now published weekly, on an adequate pecuniary foundation, and with a large and steadily increasing circulation. Its pages furnish a complete record of the movement since September, 1867, and a full report of proceedings and addresses at all principal conventions. Many of the most elaborate discussions of the principle of national responsibility to God, and other related topics, have first appeared as contributions to its columns.

For convenience of reference, and to show the dignity, importance and consistency of the principles which underlie this movement, as well as the calm, earnest and judicious spirit in which it has been carried forward, I append here the Calls for the three preceding National Conventions, held in Pittsburgh, Philadelphia, and Cincinnati, in the years 1870, 1871, and 1872 respectively, together with the resolutions adopted at each:

CALL FOR THE PITTSBURGH CONVENTION.

The Constitution of the United States makes no acknowledgment of Almighty God, the Author of national existence; nor of Jesus Christ, who is the Ruler of Nations; nor of the Bible, which is the Fountain of law and good morals, as well as of religion. This has, from the beginning, been a matter of deep regret. It may have been an oversight, but it was, and it is, both an error and an evil. It does not reflect the views of the great majority of the people upon these matters. It dishonors God. It is inconsistent with the character of nearly all our State Constitutions, and with all the precedents of our early history. It has introduced, or furthered, views and measures which are now struggling for a baneful ascendancy in State and national politics: such as, that civil government is only a social compact; that it exists only for secular and material, not for moral ends; that Sabbath Laws are unconstitutional, and that the Bible must be excluded from our public schools.

The National Association, which has been formed for the purpose of securing such an amendment to the National Constitution as will remedy this great defect, indicate that this is a Christian nation, and place all Christian Laws, Institutions and Usages in our Government on an undeniable legal basis in the fundamental law of the nation, invites, &c.

RESOLUTIONS ADOPTED AT PITTSBURGH.

Resolved, That civil government is grounded, like the family, in the principles of the nature of man as a social creature; that it has its powers and functions thus determined by the Creator, and is, therefore, like the family, an ordinance of God.

Resolved, That nations, as sovereignties, wielding moral as well as physical power, and having moral as well as material objects, are morally accountable to God.

Resolved, That the moral laws under which nations are held accountable, include not only the law written on the heart of man, but also the fuller revelation of the Divine character and will, given in the Bible.

Resolved, That it is the right of nations as such, no less than of the individuals composing them, to worship God according to the religion of Jesus Christ.

Resolved, That in order to maintain and give permanency to the Christian features which have marked this nation from its origin, it is necessary to give them authoritative sanction in our organic law.

Resolved, That the proposed amendment of our National Constitution, so far from infringing any individual's rights of conscience, or tending in the least degree to a union of Church and State, will afford the fullest security against a corrupt and corrupting church establishment, and form the strongest safeguard of both the civil and religious liberties of all citizens.

Resolved, That the present movement is not sectarian, nor even ecclesiastical, but that it is the assertion of the right, and acknowledgment of the duty of a people who believe in the Christian religion to govern themselves in a Christian manner.

CALL FOR THE PHILADELPHIA CONVENTION.

There is no political document so all-important to the American statesman and the American citizen as the Constitution of the United States. All law, all customs, all forms of administration are shaped by it. Everything in any State, corporation or business that affects a citizen in the remotest degree as to "life, liberty and the pursuit of happiness" is tested by it, and stands and works only as it agrees with it. Year by year its molding power is felt. The President, the Congress and the Courts are coming more and more into evident agreement with what is there written. Our statesmen and our whole people are learning their Americanism, as to its letter and spirit, from that great instrument. This is as it should be. This was intended from the beginning.

But, at the same time, it is a serious matter if that Constitution should be found wanting in any principle or any matter of fact. The deficiency will in due time work mischief. Error in the Constitution will work as powerfully as truth, and what is left out of it may one day be formally declared un-American. And one such serious matter there is; one unnecessary and most unfortunate omission. God and Christianity are not once alluded to: although the Constitution is itself the product of a Christian civilization, and although it purports to represent the mind of a Christian people, who in all their State Constitutions had made explicit reference to both God and religion. Hence it is that all the laws of this country in favor of a Christian morality are enacted and enforced outside of the Constitution. They rest only upon the basis of what is called Common Law. We have, strictly, no oath, no law against blasphemy, Sabbath breaking or polygamy that has any better foundation. And, as matters seem to be going, it will soon be discovered and decreed that common law is only another name for custom, which has no binding force. And then where are we? In atheism, corruption and anarchy.

The National Association which has been formed, &c.

RESOLUTIONS ADOPTED AT PHILADELPHIA.

Resolved, 1st. That this Convention of those who aim to secure a religious amendment to our National Constitution gratefully acknowledge the good providence of God in the evident progress of this cause during the past year.

2d. That, with the conviction that under God all that is wanting for its ultimate and early triumph is the publication and illustration of the facts and the principles upon which it is based, we pledge ourselves to renewed zeal in its prosecution.

3d. That this Convention renewedly calls the attention of the American people to the fact that in some of our treaties with foreign governments, which are of equal authority with the Constitution itself, we are declared to be a nation in no sense founded upon Christianity, and not (formally) unlike Mohammedans.

4th. That this Convention reiterates with an increased and solemn appreciation of their importance the following principles of moral and political philosophy, which, in substance, have been set forth by former Conventions, viz:

That civil government in the earth stands for its right of existence upon the same basis with the family, both being the appointments of the God of nature and morality, and that nations, like families, are public persons, with moral character, with rights, duties, and responsibilities.

That the continued ignoring of God and religion exposes us to the guilt of formal national Atheism.

That the nation constituted by the union of the thirteen British-American Colonies was a Christian nation, as is shown by their several Colonial histories and separate State Constitutions, and therefore it was and is no more than simple justice to the people to reflect their sentiments in the National Constitution.

5th. That, in view of the controlling power of the Constitution, in shaping State as well as National policy, it is of immediate importance to public morals and to social order, to secure "such an amendment to the Constitution as will remedy this great defect, indicate that this is a Christian nation, and place all Christian laws, institutions, and usages in our Government on an undeniable legal basis in the fundamental law of the nation;" especially those which secure a proper oath, and which protect society against blasphemy, Sabbath-breaking, and polygamy.

CALL FOR THE CINCINNATI CONVENTION.

Government is instituted for man as an intellectual, social, and moral and religious being. It corresponds to his whole nature. It is intended to protect and advance the higher as well as the lower interests of humanity. It acts for its legitimate purposes when it watches over domestic life, and asserts and enforces the sanctity of the marriage bond; when it watches over intellect and education, and furnishes means for developing all the faculties of the mind; when it frowns on profaneness, lewdness, the desecration of the Sabbath, and other crimes which injure society chiefly by weakening moral and religious sentiment, and degrading the character of a people.

Acting for such purposes, government should be established on moral principles. Moral principles of conduct are determined by moral relations. The relations of a nation to God and His moral laws are clear and definite:

1. A nation is the creature of God.
2. It is clothed with authority derived from God.
3. It owes allegiance to Jesus Christ, the appointed Ruler of Nations.
4. It is subject to the authority of the Bible, the special revelation of moral law.

In constituting and administering its Government, then, a nation is under obligations to acknowledge God as the author of its existence and the source of its authority, Jesus Christ as its ruler, and the Bible as the fountain of its laws, and the supreme rule of its conduct.

Up to the time of the adoption of the National Constitution, acknowledgments of this kind were made by all the States. They are yet made by many of the States. And in the actual administration of the national Government the principle is admitted. But the fundamental law of the nation, the Constitution of the United States, on which our Government rests, and according to which it is to be administered, fails to make, fully and explicitly, any such acknowledgment. This failure has fostered among us mischievous ideas like the following: The naticn, as such, has no relations to God; its authority has no higher source than the will of the people; Government is instituted only for the lower wants of man; the State goes beyond its sphere when it educates religiously, or legislates against profanity or Sabbath desecration.

The National Association which has been formed, &c.

RESOLUTIONS ADOPTED AT CINCINNATI.

Resolved, That the State, as a power claiming and exercising supreme jurisdiction over vast numbers of human beings, as the sovereign arbiter of life and death, and as an educating power, has necessarily a moral character and accountability of its own.

Resolved, That it is the right and duty of the United States, as a nation settled by Christians, a nation with Christian laws and usages, and with Christianity as its greatest social force, to acknowledge itself, in its written Constitution, to be a Christian nation.

Resolved, That as the disregard of sound theory always leads to mischievous practical results, so in this case the failure of our nation to acknowledge, in its organic law, its relation to God and His moral laws, as a Christian nation, has fostered the theory that government has nothing to do with religion, and that consequently laws in favor of the Sabbath, Christian marriage, and the use of the Bible in the schools, are unconstitutional.

Resolved, That we recognize the necessity of complete harmony between our written Constitution and the actual facts of the National life; and we maintain that the true way to effect this undoubted harmony is not to expel the Bible and all idea of God and religion from our schools, abrogate laws enforcing Christian morality, and abolish all devout observances in connection with Government, but to insert an explicit acknowledgment of God and the Bible in our fundamental law.

Resolved, That the proposed religious Amendment, so far from tending to a union of Church and State, is directly opposed to such union, inasmuch as it recognizes the nation's relations to God, and insists that the nation should acknowledge these relations for itself, and not through the medium of any Church establishment.

The most imposing and influential Convention yet held was that of which the following pages give the proceedings. In the number of delegates in attendance, in the variety and effectiveness of the addresses which commended the cause to enthusiastic and delighted audiences, and in the generous provision made for the prosecution of the work on an enlarged scale during the coming year, this Convention far surpassed all that have preceded it.

Wednesday, the 26th ult., the day fixed for the assembling of the Convention, was a day of spring-like mildness and beauty, a circumstance which contributed to swell the audiences at the first two sessions of the Convention. But the increasing interest of its proceedings, and the earnestness of its members and friends, were manifest in the fact that, notwithstanding an incessant snow-storm on the second day, which lasted far into the night, the attendance continued undiminished until the end. The assembly, at each of the evening sessions, numbered fully 1,500 persons, and these, with scarcely an exception, remained till a late hour with evident interest and delight.

According to the report of the Committee on Enrollment, found on page 49, *four hundred and seventy* members took seats in the Convention, and *three hundred and sixty-three* of these bore certificates of their appointment as delegates from public meetings, auxiliary societies, churches and other bodies. The students of Harvard Law School, for example, had held a meeting and appointed three of their number as delegates to New York. Thus the Convention, large as it was, represented an immensely larger constituency devoted to the cause. Nineteen States and one territory were thus represented.

A delightful feature of this, as of all previous conventions, was the harmony with which the representatives of the various denominations of Christians were able to deliberate and act together in the interests of their common Christianity and of the civil institutions which rest on it. Not a trace of denominational self-assertion, or of sectarian jealousy, was visible through the whole course of the proceedings. In fact, sectarian diversities sunk out of sight in the unity of feeling and purpose which pervaded the assembly, and the question, "Of what church is he?" was seldom asked. To every one who deplores the divisions of the Church, our work has great moral value, as it makes visible the underlying unity and essential agreement of all Christian sects, and brings them together in a holy fellowship which greatly promotes mutual acquaintance and esteem.

A similar sketch of the origin and progess of this movement, of which this is in part a condensation, was prefixed to the proceedings of the last National Convention. The reader is referred to this for additional information.

PROCEEDINGS

OF THE

NATIONAL CONVENTION,

NEW YORK,

FEBRUARY 26 AND 27, 1873.

This Convention of the friends of the movement to secure the Religious Amendment of the Constitution of the United States, met in the Large Hall of the Cooper Institute, on Wednesday, February 26, at two o'clock, P. M. The call, in response to which the Convention assembled, was as follows:

CALL FOR A NATIONAL CONVENTION.

THE QUESTION of the Bible in the Public Schools, of Sabbath Laws, and many similar questions, are now demanding attention and decisive settlement. Shall the Nation preserve the Christian features of its life? This is rapidly becoming the issue of our day.

Many thoughtful citizens view with deep concern the assaults now being made on everything of a Christian character in our civil institutions. Not only time-serving politicians and irreligious men, but eminent officers of government, and leaders among Christians, accepting the false theory that government has nothing to do with religion, coöperate in these assaults.

An appeal against the Bible in the Common Schools now lies before the Supreme Court of Ohio. It will come up for adjudication, in its regular order, sometime this winter, when a determined effort will be made to overturn the present noble school system of that State.

The Superintendent of Public Instruction of the State of New York has recently decided that the Bible, though assigned an honorable place in the State system of education when first established, and actually used for sixty years, can no longer be legally read during regular hours in any school of the State. Armed with authoritative decisions like this, the enemies of the Bible certainly will succeed unless the friends of our Common Schools awake to the dangers that threaten them, and take prompt and adequate action.

In order successfully to repel their assaults, the assailants must be met at their own point of attack. They assail the Bible in the Schools, Sabbath Laws, Laws against Polygamy, and every similar element of our Christian civilization, on the ground of their inconsistency with the Constitution of the United States, which acknowledges neither God nor the Bible, and with which everything in the actual administration of the Government should harmonize.

What shall be done? This is the momentous question now forcing itself upon the American people. It will not down. It must soon be answered in one of two ways. Which shall it be? Shall we obliterate every Christian feature from existing institutions? Or, shall we make the Constitution explicitly Christian? Shall we thrust out the Bible from our schools to make them conform to the Constitution? Patriotism and true Statesmanship answer, No! But let the acknowledgment of God and the Bible be inserted in the Constitution to make it conform to the Common Schools.

The National Association has been formed for the purpose of securing such an amendment to the Constitution as will suitably acknowledge Almighty God as the author of the nation's existence and the ultimate source of its authority, Jesus Christ as its Ruler, and the Bible as the fountain of its laws, and thus indicate that this is a Christian nation, and place all Christian laws, institutions, and usages in our government on an undeniable legal basis in the fundamental law of the land. This Association invites all citizens, who favor such an amendment, without distinction of party or creed, to meet in the HALL OF THE COOPER UNION, New York City, on Wednesday, February 26, 1873, at 2 o'clock, P. M.

All such citizens, to whose notice this call may be brought, are requested to hold meetings, and appoint Delegates to the Convention.

WILLIAM STRONG, U. S. Supreme Court,
President of the National Association.

VICE-PRESIDENTS:

His Excellency, JAMES M. HARVEY, *Governor of Kansas.*
His Excellency, SETH PADELFORD, *Governor of Rhode Island.*
The Hon. J. W. MCCLURG, *Ex-Governor of Missouri.*
The Hon. W. H. CUMBACK, *Lieutenant-Governor of Indiana.*
The Hon. WM. MURRAY, *Supreme Court of New York.*
The Hon. M. B. HAGANS, *Superior Court of Cincinnati.*
The Hon. FELIX R. BRUNOT, *Chairman of the Board of Indian Commissioners, Pittsburg, Pa.*
JOHN ALEXANDER, Esq., *Philadelphia, Pa.*
CHARLES G. NAZRO, Esq., *Boston, Mass.*
The Hon. THOMAS W. BICKNELL, *Commissioner Public Schools, Rhode Island.*
JAMES W. TAYLOR, Esq., *Newburg, New York.*
Prof. TAYLER LEWIS, LL.D., *Union College, New York.*
EDWARD S. TOBEY, Esq., *Boston.*
RUSSELL STURGIS, Jr., Esq., *Boston.*
The Right Rev. G. T. BEDELL, D.D., *Assistant Bishop of the P. E. Church, Diocese of Ohio.*
The Right Rev. G. D. CUMMINS, D.D., *Assistant Bishop of the P. E. Church, Diocese of Kentucky.*
The Rev. C. S. FINNEY, D.D., *formerly President of Oberlin College, Oberlin, O.*
The Rev. F. MERRICK, D.D., LL.D., *President of the Ohio University, Delaware, O.*
The Rev. JOSEPH CUMMINGS, D.D., LL.D., *Pres't of the Wesleyan University, Middletown, Conn.*
The Rev. A. D. MAYO, D.D., *Cincinnati.*

The Rev. T. A. MORRIS, D.D., *Bishop of the M. E. Church, Springfield, Ohio.*
The Rev. J. H. MCILVAINE, D.D., *Newark, N. J.*
Prof. O. N. STODDARD, LL.D., *Wooster University, O.*
The Rev. M. SIMPSON, D.D., *Bishop of M. E. Church.*
The Rev. J. BLANCHARD, D.D., *President of Wheaton College, Ill.*
JOHN S. HART, LL.D., *Princeton College, N. J.*
The Right Rev. JOHN B. KERFOOT, D.D., *Bishop of the P. E. Church, Diocese of Pittsburg.*
The Right Rev. F. D. HUNTINGDON, D.D., *Bishop of the P. E. Church, Diocese of Central New York.*
The Rev. T. L. CUYLER, D.D., *Brooklyn.*
The Rev. LEVI SCOTT, D.D., *Bishop of the M. E. Church, Delaware.*
Prof. JULIUS H. SEELYE, D.D., *Amherst College, Mass.*
The Right Rev. CHARLES P. MCILVAINE, D.D., LL.D., D.C.L., *Bishop of the P. E. Church, Diocese of Ohio.*
The Rev. A. A. MINER, D.D., *President of Tuft's College, Mass.*
The Rev. JONATHAN EDWARDS, D.D., *Peoria, Ill.*

GENERAL SECRETARY:

The Rev. D. MCALLISTER, 410 *West Forty-third street, New York.*

CORRESPONDING SECRETARY:

The Rev. T. P. STEVENSON, 38 *North Sixteenth street, Philadelphia.*

RECORDING SECRETARY:

The Rev. W. W. BARR, *Philadelphia.*

TREASURER:

SAMUEL AGNEW, Esq., 1126 *Arch street, Philadelphia.*

THE FOLLOWING GENTLEMEN CONCUR IN THE FOREGOING CALL:

The Hon. LORENZO SAWYER, *U. S. Circuit Court, San Francisco, Cal.*
The Hon. G. W. BROOKS, *U. S. District Court, North Carolina.*
The Hon. JULIUS ROCKWELL, *Superior Court of Massachusetts.*
The Hon. ELLIS A. APGAR, *State Sup't of Public Instruction, N. J.*
The Hon. DANIEL S. BRIGGS, *State Sup't of Public Instruction, Michigan.*
The Hon. ALONZO ABERNETHY, *State Sup't of Public Instruction, Iowa.*
The Hon. A. N. FISHER, *State Superintendent of Public Instruction, Nevada.*
The Hon. JOSIAH H. DRUMMOND, LL.D., *Portland, Maine.*
The Rev. CHARLES HODGE, D.D., *Princeton Theological Seminary, N. J.*
The Right Rev. W. M. GREEN, D.D., *Bishop of the P. E. Church, Diocese of Mississippi.*
The Rev. JOHN S. STONE, D.D., *Episcopal Theological School, Cambridge, Mass.*
The Rev. H. DYER, D.D., *Corresp. Sec. of Evang. Knowl. Society, New York.*
Vice-Chancellor J. GORGAS, *University of the South, Tenn.*
The Rev. EDMUND S. JANES, D.D., *Bishop of the M. E. Church, New York.*
The Rev. HENRY J. FOX, D.D., *Charleston, S. C.*
The Rev. THOMAS DE WITT, D.D., *Collegiate Reformed Church, New York.*
Pres't JAMES W. STRONG, D.D., *Carleton College, Minn.*
Pres't THOMAS HOLMES, D.D., *Union Christian College, Ind.*
Pres't GEO. LOOMIS, D.D., *Alleghany College, Pa.*
Pres't W. F. KING, D.D., *Cornell College, Iowa.*
The Rev. WILLIAM M. PAXTON, D.D., *First Presbyterian Church, New York.*
The Rev. WILLIAM R. NICHOLSON, D.D., *Trinity Church, Newark, N. J.*
The Rev. E. R. CRAVEN, D.D., *Newark, N. J.*
Pres't WILLIAM CAREY CRANE, D.D., *Baylor University, Texas.*
Pres't REUBEN ANDRUS, D.D., *Indiana Ashbury University.*
Pres't JOHN WHEELER, D.D., *Iowa Wesleyan University.*
Prof. J. R. W. SLOANE, D.D., *Reformed Presb. Theo. Seminary, Alleghany, Pa.*

The Rev. J. PICKETT, D.D., *Holly Springs, Miss.*
H. M. ANDERSON, Esq., *Treasurer of the University of the South, Tenn.*
Prof. LYMAN H. ATWATER, D.D., *Editor of the Presbyterian Quarterly, Princeton, N. J.*
The Rev. WILLIAM NAST, D.D., *Editor of German Publications of M. E. Church, Cincinnati, O.*
Prof. R. BETHELL CLAXTON, D.D., *P. E. Divinity School, Philadelphia.*
Pres't GEO. B. JOCELYN, D.D., *Albion College, Mich.*
Prof. J. FULLONTON, D.D., *Bates College, Maine.*
The Rev. STEPHEN H. TYNG, D.D., *St. George's Church, New York.*
The Hon. J. W. CURRY, *Member of Pennsylvania Constitutional Convention.*
The Hon. JOHN COLLINS, *Member of Penn. Consti. Con.*
Prof. H. L. SMITH, LL.D., *Hobart College, N. Y.*
Prof. THOS. SPROULL, D.D., *Reformed Presb. Theo. Seminary, Alleghany, Pa.*
Pres't J. N. RENDALL, D.D., *Lincoln University, Pa.*
Prof. S. T. WOODHULL, *Lincoln University, Pa.*
Prof. E. R. BOWER, *Lincoln University, Pa.*
Prof. T. W. CATTELL, *Lincoln University, Pa.*
Prof. J. B. RENDALL, *Lincoln University, Pa.*
Prof. J. R. JACQUES, *Illinois Wesleyan University.*
Pres't DAVID PAUL, D.D., *Muskingum College, O.*
The Hon. T. H. BAIRD PATTERSON, *Member of Pennsylvania Constitutional Convention.*

AND NUMEROUS OTHERS.

The Hon. Wm. Strong, of Washington, President of the National Association, being absent, Jno. Alexander, Esq., of Philadelphia, one of the Vice-Presidents of the National Association, called the Convention to order, and spoke as follows:

We are called together at a time of no ordinary significance. The commanding influence of our American republicanism is causing republics to be born in a day; and if constant vigilance be necessary to preserve liberty, our present national necessity is that Christian statesmanship which we have assembled together to promote. It is, therefore, no transient, sectional, or party interest that has called us to the metropolis of American influence at this time. This National Association desires to preserve and perpetuate for ourselves, our children, and for the example of all the world, the glorious inheritance which we have received from our Christian patriotic ancestors. We know from other history of the past, as well as from Holy Writ, that the nation that will not serve Him shall perish.

The Rev. A. M. Milligan, D.D., of Pittsburg, was called upon by the Chairman to lead the Convention in prayer.

A Committee on Enrollment was then appointed, as follows:

Rev. J. R. THOMPSON, Chairman; Rev. E. H. FANNING, Rev. W. H. KNOX, Rev. S. H. GRAHAM, Rev. D. B. WILLSON, Messrs. J. B. CALDWELL, A. L. KELLEY, LEWIS RENFIELD, ROBERT TAYLOR, D. CHESNUT, and JOHN LOVE.

A Committee on Permanent Organization was also appointed, as follows:

Rev. J. C. K. MILLIGAN, Chairman; Rev. GEORGE TAYLOR, Rev. ALEX. CALHOUN, and J. J. SWANWICK, Esq.

Pending the report of these Committees, the Rev. D. McAllister, General Secretary of the National Association, delivered an address, in substance as follows:

D. McALLISTER'S ADDRESS.

THE RELIGIOUS AMENDMENT MOVEMENT JUST, SEASONABLE, AND NECESSARY.

It is fitting that something should be said, at the beginning of the sessions of this Convention, in answer to the question, "For what purpose and why has this National Assembly met?" As a representative of the movement, I shall endeavor to answer this inquiry, and show that we have met to further what is right in itself, and seasonable, and necessary.

This Convention has assembled at the call of the National Association to secure the Religious Amendment of the Constitution of the United States; and the object of the Convention, like that of the Association, is to prepare the way for ultimately securing such an amendment to the Constitution as will suitably express our national acknowledgment of the authority of Almighty God, of Christ, and of the Bible. No one is committed to any form of words. A suitable acknowledgment of the nation's relation to the Supreme Ruler of nations, and His moral laws, is asked for, while it is left with the appropriate authority, either Congress or a Constitutional Convention, as the case may be, to formulate the expression.

The movement for such an amendment rests upon a fact and a principle: on the *fact* that the Government of the United States, as it is and always has been administered, stands in intimate relations with Christianity; and on the *principle* that the relations of a government to the religion of the people, as a unit, should be acknowledged in the fundamental law. The fact is indisputable. The principle is one of the most firmly established and fundamental principles of constitutional law. Let us examine each of these points, appealing to the records of history and the highest authorities in political science and jurisprudence.

The fact that our Government always has been connected with Christianity, as it never has been connected with any other religion, is so patent a fact of history as to need only to be stated. The men who came to this country and originally settled it, were, for the most part, Christians. They acknowledged Almighty God, and Christ, and the Bible. The Christian religion was the religion by whose teachings they sought to regulate all their affairs. They were of different nationalities and languages, but they were mainly of one religion—Christianity, with an open Bible. There were Swedes and Finns; there were Dutch and French settlers; there were Scotch, and Irish, and English colonists. But they were, with but comparatively few exceptions, Christian men, with their different translations of one and the same authoritative Holy Book.

Now, the religion of a people must lie at the very foundation of their nationality. Max Müller, in his lectures on the Philosophy of Religion, looking at this subject simply as a philosopher, says: "It is language and religion that make a people; but religion is even a more powerful agent than language." The history of our own nation may be cited as one of the most convincing proofs of this statement. Schelling and Hegel, expressing the conviction reached through the philosophic study of history, declare the same truth. Says Hegel, in his Philosophy of History: "Their idea of God constitutes the general foundation of a people. Whatever is the form of a religion, the same is the form of a State and its Constitution. It springs from religion."

Had Mohammedans settled this country, they would have incorporated Mohammedanism into its civil and political institutions. Had Pagans come here at first, and continued in the ascendancy, the political body formed and developed would have taken on distinctively Pagan features. The religion of a people will pervade all their relations and associations. It is the most potent of all social forces. It will inevitably control the molding of the national life. All other influences must at last succumb to it, or it must cease to be the religion of the people.

The Christians who peopled this land simply did what the settlers of any country always have done and will do. They built up institutions which were clearly and unmistakably marked with the characteristics of their religion. As Daniel Webster well said: "Our ancestors founded their government on morality and religious sentiment. They were brought hither by their high veneration for the Christian religion. They journeyed by its light and labored in its hope. They sought to incorporate it with the elements of their society, and to diffuse its influences through all their institutions, civil, political, social, and educational." They formed themselves as Christians into civil and political organizations. At first in the colonies, and then in the States, the Christian religion was acknowledged in the whole structure of government. In his commentaries on the Constitution, Justice Story remarks: "Every American colony, from its foundation down to the revolution, with the exception of Rhode Island, if, indeed, that State be an exception, did openly, by the whole course of its institutions, support and sustain, in some form, the Christian religion." After the revolution the intimate relation of the Government with Christianity still continued. Our forefathers, who called on God during their struggle, acknowledged Him in their legislative assemblies, in their schools where His word was read, and in the courts of justice where an oath was prescribed to be taken in His name. They appointed public days of fasting and thanksgiving, and placed upon their statute-books laws guarding the sacredness of the Lord's day. Again and again they declared that Christianity was part of the common law of the land.

This connection between Christianity and the administration of our Government still exists. Christian ministers are employed by Government as chaplains in public institutions. They go forth at Government's expense with our army and our navy in time of war, and still teach the truths of Christianity to soldiers and sailors in time of peace. Prayers are offered in our State legislatures and in the halls of Congress. The Bible is in our schools and the oath in our courts of justice. Laws against profanity and Sabbath desecration, though too often inoperative, are still upon our statute-books. The appointment of days for public thanksgiving, since Lincoln's time, has become the regular annual practice of the President as well as of State Governors.

Here, then, is the fact. The Government of the United States, as the government of a Christian people—a people among whom the Christian religion is altogether in the ascendancy—is to-day administered, as it always has been, in intimate connection with Christianity.

And now we come to the principle that the connection which actually exists between the government and the religion of the people should find acknowledgment in the fundamental law.

The highest authorities in Constitutional Jurisprudence are at pains to point out the distinction between the written Constitution of a nation, and that providential or historical Constitution which exists before the written instrument. Not only such authorities as De Maistre, Rothe, and Stahl, but the best writers among ourselves, such as Brownson, Hurd, Jameson, and Mulford, make this important distinction in a very clear and emphatic manner. Says the last named author, in his invaluable work entitled "The Nation:" "The Constitution of the political people has a two-fold character: there is a real and a formal Constitution. The one is the development of the nation in history—the historical Constitution; the other is the formula which the nation prescribes for its order—the enacted Constitution."

Now, a written Constitution is not a necessity of government. Up to the year 1818, the State of Connecticut had no written Constitution; nor was one framed for Rhode Island until the year 1842. If the United States Government had no written Constitution, the question as to the constitutionality of any official action would be tested by an appeal to the customs, compacts, decisions of courts, and ordinary statutes of the country. But as we have a written instrument, the appeal is made to it. And just so far as the written instrument serves its purpose as a Constitution of government, it will be a transcript of the unwritten historical Constitution of the nation. It is a dress made for the nation, and it should be made to fit. The social forces actually operating in a nation give it a certain character. They mold its institutions, determine its common law, and evolve the actual and distinctive features of the nation's life. It is the office of a written Constitution to translate these facts of the unwritten Constitution into legal language, and authenticate them. So says Judge Jameson. Mr. Mulford expresses the same thought thus: "The formal Constitution must correspond to the real. It is the order in which the people are to act, and the people must find, therefore, in the written or formal Constitution, the expression of its spirit, and its purpose must not be fettered nor perverted by it, but it must be able to act in and through it with entire freedom, in the furtherance of its aim. There must be reflected in it its own spirit, and in so far as it fails of this, it has elements of weakness or of peril."

Here, again, are the most important principles of political philosophy, thought out by able men without regard to any movement. Let the candid student of constitutional law apply them. Is it not a fact that the Christian religion is the most potent social force that ever operated among us as a people? Has it not evolved facts of a distinctively Christian character in the nation's life? Is there not, as there always has been, a vital connection betweeen our Government, in its administration, and Christianity? Do not the very demands of our opponents prove this? Is not, in other words, the real, vital, historical Constitution of our nation, Christian? And, according to the principle brought to view, should not the formal, written Constitution conform to the unwritten one, and be explicitly Christian also? If Christianity be the most powerful social force in operation in this nation, and if it have evolved, as a matter of fact, most important national features and institutions of a Christian character, as is admitted on all hands; and if it be the office of a written Constitution to translate these facts into legal language, and incorporate their authentication into itself—if it be a principle of constitutional law that the formal Constitution should correspond to the real Constitution, as the highest authorities agree in maintaining, then it seems utterly impossible to escape the conclusion that the relation which actually exists between our Government and Christianity should have expression in the written Constitution of the nation.

Such expression, however, is not found in our fundamental law. I do not wait here to show how that omission occurred. It is sufficient for us just now to have in mind the admitted fact that the national Constitution is silent as to religion, while the nation itself, as it moves on in the administration of its affairs, is not silent. Christianity has evolved and maintained the fact, in the unwritten Constitution of the nation, of prayer in the name of Christ in the nation's halls; but the written Constitution has no clause to correspond to this fact. Christianity has placed the Bible, as a fact, in the nation's courts of justice, and in the common schools; but the written Constitution does not authenticate this essential fact of our national life. Thus, to adapt to this point the language already quoted—language all the more forcible because the writer had only general principles in view, "The written or formal Constitution fails to reflect the nation's spirit in not being conformed to the real or unwritten Christian Constitution of the nation, and for this reason it has in itself elements of weakness and of peril."

Hundreds of intelligent men, when their attention has been called to this omission, while they deeply regret it, have deprecated any attempt to remedy the defect. They would rejoice, they say, had the acknowledgments we seek been made in the Constitution when first framed, but at this late day the attempt to secure them is open to the gravest objections. How forcibly does this remind us of the objection to Franklin's motion for prayers in the Convention that framed the Constitution. For nearly five weeks there seems to have been no thought of looking to God for direction in the Convention. Franklin moved that henceforth prayers be offered every morning. Mr. Sherman seconded the motion. But Mr. Hamilton and several others expressed their apprehensions that, however proper such a resolution might have been at the beginning of the Convention, it might at that late day bring on it some disagreeable animadversions. Franklin and Sherman well replied that the past omission of duty could not justify a further omission. Had the Convention not been guilty of a continued omission of an acknowledged duty, but looked to the Father of lights for guidance, we might have been spared the disasters of recent years, and the rising perils of to-day.

A continued omission on our part, to do what it is admitted ought to have been done at first, can be attended only with evil. Once more I appeal to the authority of Judge Jameson. Like the other writers to whom I have referred, he insists upon having the written Constitution conform to the unwritten Constitution of the nation. In any case in which there is a want of conformity between the formal or written and the real or unwritten Constitution, he states clearly and pointedly what should be done. And let his words be marked. They are the words of a sound lawyer. They are words of present warning. "Not only *may* the people, but, if they would insure peace with progress, they *must* by amendments cause the former to conform substantially with the latter."

Because of the failure to conform our written Constitution to the facts of the relation of our Government to Christianity, obstacles have been thrown in the way of the progress of the nation as a Christian nation. When the Constitution was adopted no one dreamed of denying that relation. But the omission of its acknowledgment in the formal Constitution soon led to its denial. Nine years after the written Constitution was framed, a treaty was ratified with Tripoli in which it is expressly stated that "the Government of the United States is not in any sense founded on the Christian religion." Justice Story tells us in his "Commentaries on the Constitution," that at the time of its adoption "an attempt to level all religions, and make it a matter of State policy to hold all in utter indifference, would have created universal disapprobation, if not universal indignation." And yet the very policy of the written Constitution is at the present time almost universally declared to be to put all religions on a level, and hold all in indifference. This is the legitimate power of silence—the potent influence of omission, of non-conformity to the real Constitution of the nation, in our fundamental law.

The same disastrous influence of this omission is seen in many practical questions of our day. Chancellor Kent and other eminent jurists decided long ago that Christianity is part of the common law of the land. This decision is now repeatedly, and in high quarters, reversed. The Supreme Court of Ohio and the Superior Court of New York City have laid down the counter-position that Christianity is not a part of our common law. Comstock, in his popular edition of "Kent's Commentaries," declares that, according to the best considered authorities, Christianity is not a part of the common law of the land. This decision is maintained all over the country by an increasing number of citizens, on the ground that the Constitution of the United States acknowledges Christianity no more than any other religion.

And now come forward the so-called "Liberals" with their demands for the discontinuance of chaplains, and of the oath, and of the Bible in the public schools, and for the abrogation of Sabbath laws, and all laws enforcing *Christian* morality, on the ground that the Constitution of the United States contains no acknowledgment of Christianity, and places all religions and no religion, irreligion, infidelity and atheism included, on a perfect equality. Their complaint is that in the actual administration of our Government all religions are *not* put upon a level, and their demand is now reiterated—and they are organizing to carry it into effect—that our whole political system shall be administered on a purely secular basis, in accordance with a written Constitution which, they boast, is untainted with any acknowledgment of Christianity.

It is useless to insist that they misinterpret the written fundamental law. However well an implied or obscurely-expressed acknowledgment of the Government's relation to Christianity might have answered heretofore, the day for every thing of this vague and uncertain kind has gone by. The nation must now declare itself. For, if it remain silent now, its written law will be made the potent weapon for enforcing the demands against our Christian civil institutions.

Nor are these opponents of the Christian institutions of the State asserting their demands in vain. Already the Bible is excluded from many of our public schools. Even prominent City and State Superintendents of Education have decided that the Holy Scriptures cannot be legally read during regular hours in our schools. Our Sabbath laws are becoming a dead letter. The theory that government has nothing to do with religion, the theory which is on every hand declared to be the theory of our national Constitution, is binding us hand and foot. The enemies of our Christian institutions set up the written Constitution before us as an insuperable barrier to our progress in Christian civilization. They defy our Christian laws of marriage and divorce, and betake themselves for refuge to the Constitution. They violate the civil safeguards of the Sabbath, and shield themselves beneath the Constitution. Elated with success, and gathering strength and boldness in their struggles, they brandish the written Constitution, and now more defiantly than ever before, assault the nation in the very citadel of its strength—the use of the Bible in its common schools. In a word, the written Constitution is to-day the spear and shield, the potent weapon both of offense and defense, of the foes of the Christian institutions of the nation.

But there is a limit to these agressions upon what is dearest and best among the institutions we have inherited. The spirit of the Christian fathers of the Republic still lives. These last sweeping demands of the enemy are rousing it from its slumber. It hears the demand for the obliteration of everything that marks our Christian character; the demand that as there is no acknowledgment of God in the Constitution, there must be none in the halls of Congress; that as there is no acknowledgment of Christianity in the written instrument, there must be none in our army or navy, or in prisons; that the Bible must be expelled from our courts and schools to make them conform to the Constitution. And already the response has begun to sound out over our States. The hundreds of delegates from the majority of the States of the Union gathered here to-day, their number every hour increasing, give expression to the deepest feelings of patriotic hearts. The answer to the "Demands of Liberalism" is an earnest and determined "No!" Our fathers founded Christian institutions. These are the sources of our prosperity, the guarantees of our liberty. For the sake of these and their blessed fruits, the written Constitution was framed. It was made for them, not they for it. The dictate of true patriotism and statesmanship is clear. The Bible must not be cast out of our schools; our Christian laws of marriage, and of the Sabbath, must not be abrogated; the oath of God must not be banished from our courts of justice, and all this to make the administration of our Government conform to the written Constitution. But, on the other hand, we shall meet the crisis that is upon us by inserting a suitable acknowledgment of God, and Christianity, and the Bible, in the written Constitution, and make it conform to our common schools and all the other essential features of our unwritten Constitution. To insure peace with progress, we *must*, by a Religious Amendment, cause the written fundamental law of the nation to conform to the Christian *facts* of our national life. This is the just, seasonable, and necessary movement, for the advancement of which we are met to-day.

At the close of this address, the Committee on Permanent Organization presented a partial report, which was completed at a subsequent session, and is as follows:

PRESIDENT OF THE CONVENTION:
HON. FELIX R. BRUNOT, *of Pittsburg.*

VICE-PRESIDENTS:

JOHN ALEXANDER, Esq., *of Pennsylvania.*
Hon. JOHN DAVIDSON, *of New Jersey.*
Hon. H. D. MAXWELL, *of Pennsylvania.*
Rev. A. A. MINER, D. D., *of Massachusetts.*
L. M. PHILIPS, Esq., *of Illinois.*
Rev. Dr. J. BANVARD, *of New Jersey.*
Rev. Dr. S. H. TYNG, *of New York.*
Rev. Dr. J. EDWARDS, *of Illinois.*
JAMES WIGGINS, Esq., *of New York.*
Rev. S. O. WYLIE, D. D., *of Pennsylvania.*
J. J. SWANWICK, Esq., *of Illinois.*
R. B. STERLING, Esq., *of Pennsylvania.*
WALTER T. MILLER, Esq., *of New York.*
DAVID BOYD, Esq., *of Ohio.*
Hon. THOS. W. BICKNELL, *Rhode Island.*
Rev. GEORGE TAYLOR, *New York.*
Rev. D. C. FARIS, *Minnesota.*
Rev. J. K. M'KALLIP, *Kentucky.*
Prof. FERRIER, *Pennsylvania.*
Rev. W. C. WILLIAMSON, *Iowa.*
JOHN RONEY, Esq., *West Virginia.*
Rev. M. S. TERRY, *New York.*
D. O. BROWN, Esq., *Maryland.*
Rev. J. R. HILL, *Michigan.*
Rev. J. P. LYTLE, *Ohio.*
Dr. S. S. GREENE, *Indiana.*
JAS. THOMPSON, Esq., *Kansas.*
Rev. C. D. TRUMBULL, *Iowa.*
J. M. M'CUTCHEON, Esq., *Colorado Territory.*

SECRETARY:
REV. SAMUEL COLLINS, *of Pennsylvania.*

ASSISTANT SECRETARIES:

Rev. N. R. JOHNSTON.
Rev. W. H. TIFFANY.
Rev. W. H. KNOX.

The President, on taking the Chair, delivered the following address:

ADDRESS OF MR. BRUNOT.

We assemble to-day, not as Republicans or Democrats, not as Protestants or Catholics, not as Methodists, Baptists, Presbyterians, or Episcopalians—not as the representatives of any political party or religious society, but as citizens of the Republic, who, ignoring differences on all points, unite in the desire to perfect the great fundamental law under which we enjoy the privileges of this meeting.

We believe that it is essential to the perfection of the Constitution of the United States that it should acknowledge God, the source of all wisdom and power, and by the recognition of Christ and the Divine law distinctly assert the Christian religion as the foundation principle of the government. We believe not only that this expression of fealty is due from the nation to the Divine source of all her prosperity, but that the Religious Amendment of the Constitution is essential to the preservation of Liberty.

We regard with feelings of the highest admiration the Constitution of the United States, and magnify the wisdom and patriotism of its framers. Their work stands unequalled among all similiar political instruments of other nations known to history. But no human work was ever absolutely perfect at its origin; neither was the Constitution of the United States. The great men who formed it recognized this fact in providing for its amendment, and amendments have already been made, the wisdom of which few will gainsay. There is hardly an educated man in America to-day who could not frame a simple clause, which, had it been originally inserted in that Constitution devised to "establish justice" and "promote domestic tranquility," would have saved the nation from a deluge of blood, and to her coffers an argosy of treasure. It is no slur upon the fathers of the Constitution that this was not done by them. It was perhaps beyond the compass of human prescience. But the omission and the result serve to illustrate the fallibility of the highest type of human wisdom, and will suggest to the most common mind that the work of the Convention of 1787 was not perfect.

That skepticism pervaded the minds of the leading statesmen of the day is undeniable. Its malign influence upon the deliberations of the Convention becomes painfully apparent when we read that the proposition of Dr. Franklin that "prayers imploring the assistance of Heaven, and its blessing upon our deliberations, be held in this assembly," received but few affirmative votes.

Their political, literary, and social relations with France were of the closest character—and the atmosphere of France was breathed by our statesmen. Her great infidel writers were then sowing the wind which seemed to that people the very breath of liberty. It grew into the whirlwind of the French Revolution. The framers of our Constitution felt the breeze, but knew not of the storm. We have seen the storm, and the awful record of it stands to our warning.

The National Association represented by this Convention fully recognizes the constitutional method by which this religious amendment is to be effected. As it is the duty of every man to labor for the good of his fellow men so far as he can do so consistently with his duty to himself and his family, so also it is his duty to labor for the perfection of his nation. In attempting this service to our country, we perform one of our chief duties to God, and in serving God we but serve our country.

If then the Constitution of the United States was not originally perfect, if its framers contemplated its future amendment, and provided a mode for amending it under which important amendments have already been made, and if we believe that a further amendment is of paramount importance and demanded by the Christian civilization of the age, and that it is our duty to labor to effect it—manifestly we assemble for a legitimate purpose, in a patriotic spirit, to pursue our object in a lawful way.

That God is the Divine author and source of all civil power accords with the opinion of the greatest men in all ages of the world. St. Paul says, "The powers that be are ordained of God," (Rom. xiii., 1,) and the words are but a summary of the teachings of Holy Writ on that subject. An eminent Church of England divine (Dr. Jortin, cited by Dr. Wines, page 85) says, "Government, both in Church and State, is of God; the forms of it are of men;" and the great truth thus tersely expressed is concurrent with the views of all distinguished writers on the subject. Nor do the most eminent writers on political science differ. Blackstone says, "Man, considered as a creature, must necessarily be subject to the laws of his Creator, for he is entirely a dependent being," and, "This will of his Maker is called the law of nature." (Sec. ii. 39 and 40.)

Vattel adopts Cicero's assertion of the fact as the motto on his title page, and in the text of his work affirms, that "*the law of nations* is no other than the *law of nature* applied to nations," and also shows that "the law of nations is the law of God," and that "the entire nation is bound to respect them in all her proceedings."

Puffendorf declares that "God, the author of the law of nature, must of right be regarded as the author of civil society, and consequently the sovereign power without which it could not exist."

Barbeyrac, an authority hardly inferior to his principal, affirms the same thing in the second paragraph of his introduction to Puffendorf, and quotes Burlamaqui and other high authorities in support.

Nor is this unanimity of sentiment confined to modern masters of political science. Plato declares that "All laws come from God; no mortal man was the founder of laws."

Heraclitus says, "All human laws are nourished by one Divine law;" and Cicero tells us that "law is nothing else than right reason, derived from the Divinity, and government an emanation from the Divine mind."

If any truth may be established by the concurrence of human authorities this truth is undoubtedly established.

Nor, in my opinion, is this view of the ultimate origin of civil power inconsistent with the affirmation as found in the Constitution of Pennsylvania—that "All power is inherent in the people." But they must be taken together, the latter being qualified by the former.

God makes no man a slave to his fellow-man. Men *are* born free and equal. Yet no man has a right to govern himself according to his own will. God creates in him a social necessity which finds its expression in government. This government is an ordinance of God; its form is of man. When two, or a hundred, or a million, come together to devise measures for mutual protection and the better pursuit of happiness, each delegates to all the others for the general good a portion of his inherent rights. They form a government with the consent of the governed; a body politic with individual attributes and powers; a State, a personality, responsible to God and to the governed. As the individual man may not rightly ignore the Divine source of power, so may not the State, which is an aggregation of divinely derived power.

That Almighty God is the source of all civil power in the State, is not only in accordance with Holy Writ and the teaching of illustrious writers on political science, but it accords with the sentiment of the American people, and the duty of acknowledging Him has ever been a part of their political and religious faith.

On the 11th day of November, 1620, the Plymouth colonists, in the cabin of the Mayflower, from which they had not landed, formed a government, which begins the record: "In the name of God. Amen." "Having undertaken for the glory of God and the advancement of the Christian religion * * * We do by these presents solemnly and mutually, in the presence of God and of one another, covenant and combine ourselves together into a civil body politic." The principles expressed in this first constitution are found in those of each of the thirteen original States.

When the Continental Congress assembled on the second day, September 6th, 1774, it was unanimously "Resolved that the Rev. Mr. Duché be desired to open the Congress with prayer," and subsequently a vote of thanks was given to Mr. Duché "for performing Divine service." When the clouds of trouble began to thicken around them we find the Continental Congress on June 12th, 1775, appointing a day of fasting and prayer. They issued a proclamation, in which occur these words: "As the Great Governor of the world, by His supreme and universal providence, not only conducts the course of nature * * * and it being at all times our indispensable duty to acknowledge his superintending power," &c.

The Declaration of Independence was made, "appealing to the Supreme Judge of the world," and "expressing a firm reliance on Divine Providence."

The ratification of the Articles of Confederation of 1778, by the original thirteen States, begins with the solemn words, "And whereas, it has pleased the Great Governor of the world to incline the heart of the legislatures we represent in Congress."

I have not had the opportunity to examine all the past and existing constitutions of the present States of the Union, but on the authority of others assert that nearly all, in some form, recognize God and the Christian religion.

When the scourge of the rebellion was upon us, the nation humbled herself before God, and acknowledged her dependence upon his power; and when the President of the United States invoked the "gracious favor of Almighty God," who in the North censured the head of the nation for his official acknowledgment of her Divine Ruler? Certainly there was no censure on this point from the South; for one of the first Confederate amendments to the Constitution was to insert the words, "invoking the favor of Almighty God."

It has been claimed that the State is a personality with individual rights, obligations, duties and responsibilities. This has been denied, but it seems to me not intelligently denied. Vattel affirms it in the words, "Nations or States are bodies politic. * * * Such a society has her affairs and her interests; she deliberates and takes resolutions in common, thus becoming a moral person, who possesses an understanding and will peculiar to herself, and is susceptible of rights and obligations." Puffendorf, Burlamaqui, Barbeyrac, Blackstone, Chitty and like authorities, agree upon this, and their opinion on such a point is usually taken as conclusive by men learned in political law.

If, then, Almighty God is the source of all political power; if the individual man is bound to acknowledge his dependence on God; if the State is a personality with obligations, responsibilities and duties; if the acknowledgment of these facts is in accordance with the general prevalent practice of the Government of the United States; if it has always accorded with the spirit and conscience of the nation and the people; if we are a Christian people—let us say so.

As I believe that the distinct assertion in the Constitution of freedom of conscience and religion is an essential to the preservation of liberty, so also I believe that the assertion of the Christian religion, the source and origin of this priceless doctrine, is of like necessity to its preservation. We assert in the Constitution the principle of freedom of conscience and popular sovereignty. Do not the American people think and act in accord with these principles? Are they not dear to every patriotic, liberty-loving citizen, and is it within the compass of human possibility to obliterate them from the great heart of the people? Who will say that because of this universal acceptance their expression in the Constitution is unnecessary? And yet there are good men who oppose the religious amendment solely upon this ground. I would give my body to be burned sooner than aid to take away from the Constitution its guarantees of freedom of conscience in religion. I see that Constitution stand like a tree with branches, upon which are inscribed the relations they hold to a great vital principle at its heart—beautiful in its branches—beautiful in their symmetrical combination; but it is to the eye a cut tree drawing its sustenance from artificial sources. And yet its roots are deeply planted in, and its sustenance drawn from, the soil of Christianity from which it sprang. I would inscribe Christianity upon its sturdy roots, and upon its massive trunk Almighty God, by whose supreme and gracious power alone it may stand perpetually for the enlightenment of the nations.

Gentlemen of the Convention, I thank you for the honor you have been pleased to confer upon me. That the course of your deliberations, and the conclusions you may reach, will comport with the dignity and importance of the object for which you are assembled, I cannot doubt; and in this belief I assume the honorable place you have given me, assured of your aid in my efforts rightly to perform its duties, and your forbearance should I in some things fail.

A Committee on Resolutions was next appointed, as follows: Rev. J. Edwards, D. D., *Chairman*, Rev. A. A. Miner, D. D., Rev. M. S. Terry, Hon. John Davidson, Hon. H. D. Maxwell, Rev. J. P. Lytle, and Rev. T. P. Stevenson.

The Executive Committee of the National Association was appointed a Committee on Business of the Convention.

In pursuance of the programme previously arranged, the Rev. Dr. E. R. Craven, of Newark, N. J., then delivered an address on "The Religious Defect of the Constitution."

ADDRESS OF DR. CRAVEN.

Mr. President: I yield to no man in the love I bear my country, and in my admiration of the great men who formed our Constitution, and of the Constitution they formed. That instrument I regard as one of the masterpieces of human workmanship. But no human work is perfect. In my humble judgment there is a defect in that glorious instrument, and I am here as the friend of my country to declare it, and to plead for its correction. That defect is its failure to recognize the sovereignty of Jehovah over the NATION.

By *defect* we mean not mere *lack*, but the lack of that which is proper to a person or thing. In declaring that the Constitution is defective in that it does not recognize the sovereignty of Jehovah, it is contemplated that it should contain such a recognition; and to the establishment of this fact my argument will first be directed.

Before proceeding to the argument, it is proper that certain preliminary remarks should be made. And first, as to the *assumptions* of the argument. I assume that a personal God exists, and that the Bible contains a revelation of His will. My argument this afternoon is with those only who admit these facts. I may further state that in affirming that our Constitution is defective in the respect mentioned, it is not affirmed that we are not a religious people; on the contrary, the assumption of the fact that we are such a people essentially underlies the position that we ought to acknowledge Jehovah as our king; were it otherwise, such an acknowledgment would be hypocrisy. Nor is it implied that the framers of our Constitution, or a majority of them, were not religious men; good men sometimes make mistakes. Nor is it implied that, so long as the defect exists, we are discharged from the duty of allegiance. The fact that a father may be an atheist does not discharge the children from the divinely-imposed obligation to honor him; and it should also be remembered that it was to a *heathen* emperor that an Apostle exhorted Christians to subject themselves, declaring that the powers that be are ordained of God. With these preliminary remarks, I proceed to my argument.

I. The Constitution should contain a recognition of the sovereignty of God.

What is the Constitution? Of course a complete definition of this instrument cannot be expected on this occasion, nor am I the person to give it. All I shall attempt to do is, to present it in one of its aspects. Justice Story has set forth in his great commentary that it is not "a mere compact, treaty, confederation of the States composing the Union," but that it is "a form of government which, having been ratified by a majority of the people in all the States, is obligatory upon them, *as the prescribed rule of the sovereign power*, to the extent of its provisions." (*Story on the Constitution*, B. III., ch. III., § 350.) It is then manifestly, according to this distinguished Judge, *the utterance of the nation as a nation;* and it, together with its amendments, is the only such utterance. But this, in view of the circumstances in which it was framed and adopted, involves two things: *first*, that it is a formal declaration before the world of the fact of completed, undivided nationality; and, *second*, that its adoption was an assumption of the prerogatives and duties of such nationality.

But what is a *Nation?* It is not, as some suppose, a mere aggregation of individuals bound together by social compact; it is a company of *related* individuals, an organism—a body having many members and pervaded by a common life. The individuals who compose it, though they may have individual differences, have certain common characteristics—physical, mental and moral—common hopes and aspirations. Cast a million of men, women and children, not already bound by national ties, into such a country as the Valley of the Mississippi, and you have not a *nation*. The mass of individuals may indeed contain the germ of a nation, but in order to nationality they must be placed under a process of discipline: they must be placed under *special* discipline in order to the production of some special form of life. In this process, the weak and those who have no aptitude for the special form of life to be produced will be winnowed out; the strong in whom the aptitude exists will be developed, and not only so, but they will be bound together by common efforts and by common trials; and in the end a *nation* will come forth—an organism fitted to take into itself and to assimilate the individuals who may afterwards be brought into connection with it. Nations are *growths*, not mere *voluntary associations*.

Of such organisms, God is the alone author. It lies upon the surface of the Bible, in reference to a nation, that He plants, He disciplines, He guides, He gives prosperity, He chastises, He plucks up, He destroys. These declarations of His word are exemplified throughout the whole course of history—and in the history of no nation more completely than that of our own. It needs not that, before this audience, I should recite God's dealings with us. How in the beginning He formed this land for the reception of a free people, and kept it secret till the time for the establishment of this people had come. How in another continent He prepared the seed that here was to be planted; how in process of time He brought our fathers here and planted them in thirteen colonies; how by discipline, by exposure to hardness, to struggle with the elements of nature, with savage beasts, and with more savage men, He at once bound them together in separate brotherhoods, and developed in them the spirit of courage, energy, self-reliance, independence, in short, trained and hardened them into republics; how, in process of time, by the struggles, the fires, the twistings, the hammerings of the revolution and following events, He bound together, twisted, welded into one living mass, the different fibres He had separately formed, and thus formed and established this nation, in the home He had previously prepared for it.

The adoption of the Federal Constitution was not the adoption of a social compact forming a nation—*that* God had formed; it was the solemn declaration before the other nations of the earth of the fact of perfected nationality, and the solemn assumption of the prerogatives and duties of such nationality. This declaration, this assumption, were not made in the Declaration of Independence; that was the declaration of thirteen affiliated colonies. They were not made in the Articles of Confederation; that was a treaty between thirteen mutually independent States. It was not until the period of the adoption of the Constitution that the Providential work of forming the *nation* was completed; and it was then, and not until then, that the declaration before the world of the fact of one undivided nationality was made.

It was meet that, at such a time, the *Nation* God had formed and blessed, should, in the instrument in which they assumed what He had given, formally declare their gratitude and their allegiance to Him as their Sovereign. Nay, further, I ask, in view of the preamble of the Constitution, which is in these words: "We, the people of the United States, in order to form a more perfect union, establish justice, insure domestic tranquility, provide for the common defense, promote the general welfare, and secure the blessings of liberty to ourselves and our posterity, do ordain and establish this Constitution for the United States of America"—in view of this preamble in which is set forth as the object of the adoption of the Constitution the securing of the very blessings which in His Scriptures Jehovah declares that He holds in His own hand,—in view of this preamble I ask if, at such a moment, the failure to recognize His sovereignty was not an ignoring of that sovereignty, if it was not tantamount to the claim that by their own wisdom they had been guided, that by their own strength they had been established, that by their own wisdom and strength they were to attain unto, and retain further prosperity.

And still further, we all know, as has been set forth to-day by our President, that at the period of the adoption of the Constitution the principles that were then moving France were widely disseminated throughout our own land. Many of our best men believed that religion was a matter that concerned merely the individual; that nations as such were mere associations, the creatures of social compact, owing allegiance only to themselves. I verily believe that, under this erroneous idea, a recognition of the Divine sovereignty—nay, the bare mention of the name of God—was excluded from the instrument.

II. But does this Constitution fail to recognize the Divine sovereignty? This question brings me to the second division of my argument.*

That it does so would seem to be evident upon a mere perusal. The name of God does not appear in it. The preamble, where we naturally look for such a recognition, impliedly claims the wisdom and power by which we stand for the people. There are those, however, who contend that such a recognition, though not directly, is impliedly made. The arguments of these I shall briefly consider.

1. It is contended by some that such a recognition is impliedly made, in that the Constitution requires an *oath* as a qualification for office. An *oath*, say they, is an appeal to the Supreme Being, and the requirement of an oath is an implied recognition of His supreme authority.

In answer, I remark: *First*, That even though the Constitution require an oath in the true and proper meaning of that term, such requirement does not necessarily involve a recognition of the Divine Sovereignty over the *nation*. A voluntary association, ignoring all allegiance to God as an *association*, may still deem it wise, before entrusting an individual with important interests, to bind his conscience by an appeal to a Being whose authority over him as an *individual* he recognizes. But, *secondly*, The Constitution does not require an *oath*, *in the true and proper meaning of that term*. The *oath* that the Constitution prescribes to be taken by the President of the United States is in these words: "I do solemnly swear (or affirm) that I will faithfully execute the office of President of the United States, and will, to the best of my ability, preserve, protect and defend the Constitution of the United States"—you naturally expect to hear following, the time-honored formula, "So help me God," but it is not there; and a subsequent provision forbids that it should be there, viz.: in Art. VI., Sec. 3, where, immediately after the requirement that all officers "shall be bound by oath or affirmation to support the Constitution," it is provided that "*no religious test* shall ever be required as a qualification to any office or public trust under the United States." Now, Mr. President, I do not deny that any man in taking the oath prescribed by the Constitution, may, if he so choose, make an appeal to the Supreme Being; but, manifestly, under the force of that proviso, he need not make such an appeal unless he chooses—the Constitution does not require it. On Tuesday

* The substance of the following portion of this argument may be found in a tract written by the speaker, and published by the *Christian Statesman* in 1868.

next another inauguration is to take place. President Grant may, if he so choose, appeal to God ; but even as he takes the oath required, he may proclaim himself an *atheist*, and there is no power on earth that can stay his inauguration. The Constitution does, in terms, require an *oath*, but by the proviso quoted it degrades it to the low platform of a solemn promise—the oath that it *requires* is emasculated.

2. In the second place, it is contended that the Constitution impliedly recognizes the Divine authority in that it recognizes *Sunday* (in a parenthesis !) as a day retired from business. (See Art. I., Sec. 7.)

The answer is patent. In the *first* place, even though the proviso contemplates the *divinely* imposed obligation of the Sabbath, it would not, necessarily, imply a recognition of the sovereignty of God over the *nation*. A voluntary association, if it act wisely, will make provision not to interfere with the *personal* obligations of its members. But, *secondly*, the proviso does not necessarily contemplate the divinely imposed obligation of the Sabbath even upon individuals. An atheist would vote for a law forbidding murder, without thereby recognizing even the existence of Him who ordained "Thou shalt not kill." It is evident, upon merely natural considerations, that man needs a rest day. The *seventh* day, as a rest day, is, to say the least, as good as any other. Even an atheistic legislator in making provision for a rest day, and finding the division of time into weeks already established, would, if he acted wisely, adopt the arrangement already made to his hand.

3. Again, it is contended that the (so-called) concluding clause of the Constitution does most expressly recognize the sovereignty of the Lord Jesus. The clause is in these words: "Done in Convention, by the unanimous consent of the States present, the seventeenth day of September, *in the year of our Lord* one thousand seven hundred and eighty-seven, &c."

Now I remark, in the *first place*, that manifestly this clause forms no part of the Constitution as adopted by the PEOPLE. It is merely an attesting clause adopted by the Convention that framed the instrument ; the *People* did not adopt the attesting clause of the *Convention*. But, still further, the words *in the year of our Lord*, formed no part of the clause as adopted by the Convention. Madison, in his Minutes of the Convention, gives the clause *as adopted*, in this abbreviated form, "Done in Convention by the unanimous consent of *the States* present the 17th of December, &c. In witness whereof we have hereunto subscribed our names." [*See Elliott's Debates, Vol. I., p.* 317 (*Madison's Minutes*) *; also, Vol. V., p.* 555 (*Madison's Debates*).]*

We have now considered all the grounds upon which it is contended that the sovereignty of Jehovah over the nation is recognized in the Federal Constitution. The points at issue, so far from manifesting the truth of the fact claimed, serve only to make more manifest the utter exclusion of any mention even of the existence of God in the instrument.

---

* The history of the clause is briefly as follows: (see *Elliott's Debates*, Vol. V., *Madison's Debates*, p. 555.) The Constitution was not adopted by the unanimous vote of all the members present in the Convention, although it was approved by the majorities of the representatives of all the States. It was feared that the dissenting members would refuse to sign it. The clause *as adopted* was moved by Dr. Franklin for the purpose of securing a unanimous signature. Madison comments as follows: "This ambiguous form had been drawn up by Mr. Gouverneur Morris, in order to gain the dissenting members, and put into the hands of Dr. Franklin, that it might have the better chance of success." Manifestly, that which was in the mind of the Convention when they considered and passed the clause, was the first portion and not the mode of signifying the date. The blank was subsequently filled out in compliance with prevailing custom, probably by the clerk.

But it is argued by some that any defect in our Constitution is, in effect, healed by the fact that prayers were daily offered in the Convention that framed it. Would, sir, that such had been the case—but, alas! it was not. It is generally believed that prayers were offered; the statement that such was the fact is made in many of our histories. I well remember the thrill that passed through me, when, in my boyhood, I read the account that is still current. How, after many days of fruitless wrangling, Franklin rose in the Convention, and after a noble speech offered the resolution that thereafter prayers imploring Divine guidance should daily be offered; how Washington, advancing with glowing face from the President's chair, declared that the offering of prayer was what was needed, and then put the question, which was unanimously carried; how, on the following morning, a venerable minister led the Convention in devotion at the Mercy-seat; and how the clouds of discord passed away, and the body in unbroken harmony went on to a glorious conclusion. I verily believed that such was the blessed truth, until in my manhood I discovered, to my surprise and mortification, that the only elements of truth in the narrative were that Franklin had made the speech and offered the resolution. A full account of the transaction is given in *Madison's Debates* (*Elliott's Debates*, Vol. V., pp. 253–255), which, as it is short, I will read, the more especially as the speech of Franklin, which is still preserved in his own handwriting, shows the opinion of that wisest among the fathers of the Republic, of the relation of a nation to God.

MR. PRESIDENT: The small progress we have made, after four or five weeks' close attendance and continual reasonings with each other, our different sentiments on almost every question, several of the last producing as many *noes* as *ayes*, is, methinks, a melancholy proof of the imperfection of the human understanding. We indeed seem to *feel* our own want of political wisdom, since we have been running all about in search of it. We have gone back to ancient history for models of government, and examined the different forms of those republics, which having been originally formed with the seeds of their own dissolution, now no longer exist; and we have viewed modern states all round Europe, but find none of their constitutions suitable to our circumstances.

In this situation of this Assembly, groping, as it were, in the dark to find political truth, and scarce able to distinguish it when presented to us, how has it happened, sir, that we have not hitherto once thought of humbly applying to the Father of Lights to illuminate our understandings? In the beginning of the contest with Britain, when we were sensible of danger, we had daily prayers in this room for the Divine protection. Our prayers, sir, were heard—and they were graciously answered. All of us who were engaged in the struggle must have observed frequent instances of a superintending Providence in our favor. To that kind Providence we owe this happy opportunity of consulting in peace on the means of establishing our future national felicity. And have we now forgotten that powerful friend?—or, do we imagine we no longer need its (His) assistance? I have lived, sir, a long time; and the longer I live, the more convincing proofs I see of this truth, *that* GOD *governs in the affairs of men.* And, if a sparrow cannot fall to the ground without His notice, is it probable that an empire can rise without His aid? We have been assured, sir, in the Sacred Writings, that, "except the Lord build the house, they labor in vain that build it." I firmly believe this; and I also believe, that without His concurring aid we shall succeed in this political building no better than the builders of Babel; we shall become divided by our little, partial, local interests, our projects will be confounded, and we ourselves shall become a reproach and a by-word down to future ages. And, what is worse, mankind may hereafter, from this unfortunate instance, despair of establishing government by human wisdom, and leave it to chance, war, and conquest.

I therefore beg leave to move,

That henceforth, prayers, imploring the assistance of Heaven and its blessing on our deliberations, be held in this Assembly every morning before we proceed to business; and that one or more of the clergy of this city be requested to officiate in that service.

[The speaker then read the abstract of the debate in the Convention on Franklin's motion, and the following remark of Madison, "After several unsuccessful attempts for silently postponing this matter by adjournment, the adjournment was at length carried without any vote on the motion." He also read the endorsement made by Franklin on the MS. of the speech (*Works of Franklin*, by Sparks, Vol. V., p. 155), "The Convention, except three or four persons, thought prayers unnecessary!"]

There are some who argue that there cannot be an important religious defect in our Constitution, since God has given us unexampled prosperity under it. These take for granted what manifestly is not true, that God is always swift to punish. Why, sir, even the heathen recognized the fact that "the mills of the gods grind slowly." God *forbears* to punish. Often He forbears through long years that He may give space for repentance—that through chastisement He may lead to reformation. And, when chastisement has proved ineffective, He often still forbears to destroy those who resist Him, permitting them to go on to high degrees of prosperity, that His own power and sovereignty may be made more brightly manifest in their ultimate destruction. Let us not forget that He permitted the tower of Babel to reach a mountain height before He confounded the language of the builders.

And here, sir, I would remark that the reference by Franklin to Babel is to me one of fearful significance. Our Constitution was framed as was Babel, to secure the blessings of union—that we might not be scattered abroad. Let us not forget that the troubles which recently afflicted us—the storm that burst like a tornado over this land, carrying sorrow to every home, arose from *confusion of language* in regard to our fundamental instrument. Methinks, God then chastised us that He might teach us true wisdom. One of the blessed effects of our civil war was that it brought this whole people to the feet of our God with the acknowledgment of Him as Sovereign. In mercy He heard our prayers, He removed His chastising hand, He spared our union, He has given us space for repentance. It should be the first work of our gratitude and our loyalty to correct our Constitution—that formal utterance of the nation before the world—which ignores His authority. Let us beware lest a forbearing and insulted God arise to destroy us.

I know that in the judgment of many it is well nigh treason to speak as I have spoken. Sir, I repeat the remark with which I began this address, that I yield to no man in love for my country, but I regard it as no mark of love to shut my eyes to the fact of disease in a loved object. It is no mark of love to wife or mother for a man to shut his eyes to the fact that a cancer is preying upon her vitals—nay, love, guided by true wisdom is quick to perceive the fact, and, if need be, apply the knife for its eradication. I think I perceive vital defect in our Constitution, and in love I proclaim the fact as in order to its removal. O! that the nation taught by the past, moved by gratitude and loyalty to Him who has blessed us, would inscribe Jehovah's name upon our banner that we might escape His future judgments, that we might be that happy people whose *acknowledged* God is the Lord.

At the close of Dr. Craven's address, it was resolved that the sessions of the Convention be from 9 to 12 o'clock in the morning; from 2 to 5 in the afternoon; and in the evening from 7½ o'clock until such time as the Convention may see fit to adjourn.

Adjourned to meet in the evening at 7½ o'clock.

EVENING SESSION.

The Convention having re-assembled, the President invited Dr. Stephen H. Tyng to open the meeting with prayer.

The large audience present was then addressed by the Rev. J. H. McIlvaine, D.D., of Newark, N. J.

DR. McILVAINE'S ADDRESS.

The presence of so large an assembly here to-night indicates an increase of interest in this cause, for which I am profoundly thankful.

There are some who think there is a sufficient recognition of God, and of Christianity, in the fact that the Constitution was dated "in the year of our Lord, 1787." But the expression, strictly considered, does nothing more than declare the era of the world's history in which the Constitution was framed. Of precisely the same force are the expressions, "The Julian Era," or "The Chaldean Era," in documents written in those ages. The question is whether this is a sufficient acknowledgment of the authority of the Christian religion, and that question I am willing to leave to the judgment of sensible men, without further argument.

The question is: Shall we have such an amendment as shall suitably acknowledge God, and not have our Constitution devoid of all mention of His name as it now is? In considering this, I would notice *the vast significance and influence of national acts as compared with individual acts.* An act of the government is a national act; as the making treaties, declaring war, the making of peace, and the like. Now consider for one moment, the immense significance of such acts as these; what immense influences they exert upon the minds and destinies of the people. Let our Government declare war on any foreign nation, and every individual becomes involved in it, and in the miseries that may flow from it. These influences reach all over the nation, extending to every family, and to every individual. *Any* act of the National Legislature is far-reaching in its influence. Can you think that the omission of any needed act can be of less significance than the doing of it? The omission of what should be is as far-reaching as the doing of what should not be done. It must be of immense significance; it cannot be otherwise. Therefore, the importance of the subject calling us together seems to me to be evident to every mind.

There is an evident necessity of doing something to reach the object at which we aim. Here we are, a great Christian nation. That it is so may be seen from the fact that from Christian principle we have our laws and our institutions of education, and all our hopes of future prosperity. [Applause.] And yet with all such basing of the nation on Christian morality—so long as the Constitution stands as it now is—Christian morality is not recognized distinctly. There are different moralities in the world, and theories of morals, as Turkish, Pagan, and others, that differ from the Christian system of morals. There is something that may be called a Mormon system or theory of morals, differing greatly from the Christian system of morals. I ask : on what authority in the Constitution of the United States can distinct inculcation of Christian morality be enacted? I cannot find any such authority in the Constitution as it now is.

In this country, though there is far greater Christian light here than anywhere else, religion and politics have been unlawfully divorced, and this divorcement is favored by the Constitution of the United States. The tendency seems to be, all the time, for men to drift farther and farther away from religious influences the more they are connected with politics. The roots of morality are in religion. It is not possible that there can be any deep-rooted morality in an irreligious people. There must be connection and communication between religion and politics. Politicians separate from religious action are separate from moral influences, and they fall inevitably into a state of mind in which they say to themselves, "As members of the family, as men of business, we ought to make some profession of religion;" but in political life there is no need of religion, and so they banish religion from their modes of political action! Therefore it is notorious that men in office are guilty of breaches of morality which they would not be guilty of in private life—men that bear comparatively good reputations in private life are unprincipled in public life.

This leads me to seek the cause why the Constitution leaves out all mention of God? I do not think that the framers of it were all infidels, or hated morality. But because the people came from countries where the church and the state had been united in such a manner as to degrade and oppress ; and the representatives of the people having such powerful prejudices guarded against such union by leaving out of the expression of the national life all reference to the church. All men know that such union is not our aim. We want no union of church and state. [Cheers.] Now, in guarding this point, our fathers went to the opposite extreme. I cannot characterize it in any other way. In avoiding mention of the church, they avoided all mention of religion, and this failing has exerted a corrupting influence on our political morality. It has given birth to the common remark, "We must not bring religion into politics. The only way to keep religion pure is to keep it separate from politics." But it does not seem to have entered into the mind of men that this is a two-edged sword which cuts both ways. When we have withdrawn religion from politics to keep religion pure, what is to keep politics pure thus separated from religion? [Prolonged applause.] When we have taken religion out of our political life, the salt is taken away, and it is left to irretrievable corruption. [Applause.]

Apart altogether from the church, if there had never been any church in the world, and never was to be any, the nation is the creature of God, and is bound to acknowledge His moral government. [Applause.] And He rewards the nation for obedience, and punishes it for disobedience. And when in our national acts we fail to recognize our national obligations to God, it seems to me that we *sin* as a nation, and drag down ourselves into political demoralization.

There is an immense difference between the morality of the people and the morality of our politics. This difference is lamentable; and it cannot continue long in the direction it is now going. The whole nation is affected by such public morality. The reason is, there is no government in the world where the political sphere of life is so great as it is here. Every man here is, more or less, a politician. A greater number of persons are deeply interested in politics than in any other country in the world. Political influences are therefore exerted in every family, in every home, and in every heart. Now, if our political life becomes demoralized—as it threatens to become—how long will the common life of the people continue pure? If a man will commit perjury in political life, how long will it be before he will swear falsely in business matters? How long will corruption be confined to the political sphere of life? It cannot be confined there, but will permeate all parts of the people's life, and more rapidly in this country than in any other country in the world. A despot wants moral men to be his officers, however selfish he may be himself. He wishes to have good men in his service. But in this country, where all is different, if false ideas of political morality extend, as they seem almost destined to do; if the maxim be generally accepted, "All is fair in politics;" if you send such men for legislators as have been generally sent, and they act as they have generally acted, our ruin is sure and speedy.

With these remarks I leave the matter to be discussed by others better qualified. In closing let me say, that to my mind it seems the most preposterous thing for a great nation like ours to attempt to carry on its government under a Constitution which contains no reference to God or moral law and Christianity. I expect that soon this nation will rise, as one man, and demand this amendment, *because they cannot live any longer without it.* [Great applause.]

The Rev. Dr. S. H. Tyng, Sr., was introduced by the President, and delivered the following address:

DR. TYNG'S ADDRESS.

Mr. President, and my Christian Friends—for so I will address this large assemblage:—We have been called to consider a great Christian question. We are assembled as a company of the sincere representatives of the word and authority of the Lord Jesus Christ. This is as really a distinctively Christian assembly, as if it were gathered especially for the purpose of prayer.

The great question before us seems to me, as I have read and listened to its discussion, to have but one side. I have heard nothing on the other but arbitrary objections, and rude and reproachful sneers. We may be considered in this relation as men of one idea. But it is an idea of unspeakable grandeur and of vast importance. We propose that the constitution of a Christian land and government shall openly and distinctly acknowledge the authority of Him who is its proper and acknowledged Ruler, whom in all the acts of authority they habitually designate as "OUR LORD."

For the propriety and duty of this I have read and listened to the most effective, intelligent and unanswerable arguments. In opposition to them, so far as I have heard, there are three classes of objectors, from neither of which have I heard one reply which has appeared to me worthy of a moment's thought.

The *first* acknowledges the propriety of our demand in principle, but says it is unnecessary because, by implication at least, in its date and in some of its appointments, the Constitution already acknowledges the divine authority, and the special authority of the Lord Jesus Christ. I am grateful for the concession ; but I reply that an open, distinct profession of this acknowledgment is so much the more important that the character and authority of an instrument which is thus conceded to be accidentally or intuitively right, in an underlying principle, should make that distinctive and most important principle an open and indisputable avowal. And however adequate the influence might have been in an earlier period and with a far smaller community, amidst the gathered objections and hostilities of our now immensely extended nation and our excited period, it is of infinite consequence that the nation shall openly and candidly declare in its Constitution that divine authority which it is conceded does actually underlie its whole administration of power, and its avowed aspect and purpose as a community. This first class agree with us in our fundamental desire, but separate from us only in the expediency of a time, and a form for its accomplishment. We can hardly regard this class as a class of opposers.

The *second* class concede that there is no such acknowledgment of divine authority in the Constitution as we desire, and defend the omission. Their view seems to be, that a political document should be kept clear from all religious reference or expression. They are not unbelievers in Christianity. Perhaps they regret, in some cases, that there was not some such expression as we desire incorporated in the Constitution at its outset. But they are now opposed to any alteration of the venerable instrument for this purpose. We have simply to reply, it is never too late to do right. However old an error may be there cannot be a greater mistake than to perpetuate it. The avowed principle that Christian influence, morality and truth are not to be allowed to affect public justice or law can never be maintained but by absolute enemies to Christianity in itself. And these objectors we cannot allow ourselves to number among the fearful array of avowed infidels in Christian truth.

But the *third* class is composed of just these infidels. They meet us with their own only weapons of sneers, derision, reproach and blasphemy. We have seen and read much of them of late. They call us "God in the Constitution party." I am free to accept the title. I am just that. I belong to the "God in the church" party, to the "God in the household" party, to the "God in the heart" party. The divine authority, the name and glory of Jesus, I wish to have everywhere acknowledged and revered.

This is a class of objectors to whom I would say, "We are not careful to answer you concerning this matter." When I meet with low personal abuse, vulgar derision and blasphemous imprecations upon the holy name whereby we are called, I shall withdraw from all association with such, or reference to them. We do not ask their help. We do not fear their hostility. We shall not shrink from the performance of our duty for their coarse reproaches. We are the party who would acknowledge the authority of God, and the name of Jesus, at all times, in the nation, in the community, in the family, in the individual life.

I would say to you, my friends, we must pursue this great purpose with unshrinking fidelity. Agitate! Agitate! Agitate! We are perfectly sure of an ultimate triumph. We are on the side which must conquer. If not in our generation, yet in the generations which will come after us—whoever may oppose.

The particular formula in which this desired amendment to the Constitution shall be expressed, with most effect and propriety, I am free to say we may not yet have attained. It needs some special inspiration of wisdom, perhaps, to frame a perfectly successful utterance. God will give that to us in His own time.

We are not here assembled to make this amendment. That belongs to the people themselves, through their appointed representatives. But we are arrayed to promote it, to awaken attention to its importance, to arouse public sentiment in favor of its adoption. And for this we are to go on in our work, indifferent to reproach, careless of mere hostile objections.

Therefore I say, Agitate! Agitate! Agitate the demand for this great principle of acknowledgment. Generations after will need it as much as we; and whatever increase or advance in wisdom we may gain in our period of labor we will bequeath to those who come after us, that they may carry forward the great contest for the Saviour's glory, till the end be completely attained. If you and I are to lie down in the grave before this great work is done, let us leave our testimony to our sons, and our sons' sons, with the charge to accomplish in their day this great glory of our land. Great and lasting principles grow slowly, but surely. And God, who gave us our glorious country, and prepared and guided our forefathers for its prosperous establishment, will maintain his own honor and government in it.

I have no doubt of the glorious government of God over all the earth; nor of the future unlimited establishment and display of the dominion of Jesus Christ our Lord, over the whole world for which He died and which He has redeemed by His death. And I have no doubt either, that this, my beloved country, will stand forth high and honored among the agencies which shall bring on the last reign of holiness and glory. And for that exalted government, and for all that conduces to its maintenance and establishment we are here engaged, in the all-important question and purpose, which have brought us here this day.

Let reproaches come. They are of little consequence. Infidelity is but a puddle, the result of a temporary shower. Truth, the Truth of God, the Truth of Jesus, is an everlasting spring, flowing from the love and wisdom of God, which will roll onward and spread itself abroad, until its waters fertilize the whole earth; and an eternity to come shall be filled with the glory which has been gathered from this earth restored to God, and sanctified and saved by the power and truth of that Glorious Saviour whom He hath crowned Lord of Lords and King of Kings.

The Rev. Dr. Edwards, Chairman of the Committee on Resolutions, reported a series of resolutions. For these, as adopted by the Convention after discussion, see page 41.

Dr. A. A. Miner, President of Tuft's College, Mass., was then introduced, and spoke for about fifty minutes, on the "Influence of Silence in Regard to Fundamental Law," substantially as follows:

ADDRESS OF DR. MINER.

If the men and women of this country were asked, what of all the facts and principles that enter into our national life are most important, ninety-nine in a hundred would answer, the facts and principles of Christianity. These, they would say, were operative when the nation had birth, and have ever since continued operative, in various degrees of purity. Thus they regard Christianity as essentially our fundamental law. At the same time they are aware that what we call our fundamental law, the Constitution of these United States, is utterly silent in regard not only to the author of Christianity, but to the very being of a God; and this silence, they quite generally think, it would be impolitic, even hazardous, to break. They rely on Christianity to conserve the nation's interests, and promote its welfare, but think it must be done quietly, not overtly. I cannot but ask, how can it be wise to do covertly what it would be unwise, even hazardous, to do openly?

What is the origin and what the tendency of this silence in regard to our essential law? It must not be forgotten that the early colonies were deeply and strongly religious. Some of them had even identified citizenship and church-membership. However jealous of their own rights of conscience, they had learned scarcely the rules of toleration as a principle, and did not hesitate to inflict various disabilities, rising sometimes to gravest persecution, upon those who could not see with their eyes and hear with their ears.

From such causes there arose an exceeding jealousy of civil interference in matters of religion. Those who had been trained under persecution at home, strengthened by accessions of men repelled by church and state tyranny abroad, constituted a host justly opposed to any union of church and state under the new polity. Divisions of the church had become more numerous, and it was properly felt that there must be no preference given to one church over another in the national charter. How to secure the equal rights of all, otherwise than by utter silence in regard to Chistianity itself, they did not discover. And so error was shielded and the chasm bridged.

That French Atheism and English Deism had exerted their baneful influence on American thought, there can be no doubt. The number of free-thinkers in the country was absolutely great, though it was relatively small; and an undue proportion of such men were embraced in the national councils. What covert influence their personal rejection of Christianity had in determining the method of securing equal rights, it is, perhaps, impossible to say; but that the silence determined upon did not mean the rejection of Christianity, but did mean rather the perfect toleration of the various sects, seems quite clear. Had it been understood that the former was the meaning, there would have been such an outcry throughout the length and breadth of the land as would have prevented the ratification of the Constitution by the people.

Nor in case the silence of the Constitution had meant a rejection of Christianity, whould there have arisen at once those Christian observances and usages, the appointment of chaplains, and of days of thanksgiving and the like, which have continued to our own time.

But those who esteemed Christianity as above all price, and who yet favored silence in the interests of toleration, doubtless reasoned on this wise: "The great body of the people are Christian. What the people are, their Government will substantially be. If they are Christian, Christianity will utter itself in the State Constitutions; it will modify criminal law; it will temper by a higher and broader justice the whole body of the laws. We need not, therefore, be anxious about any recognition of Christianity in the Constitution itself." This surely is plausible; but is it sound? If the Christianity of the people naturally embodies itself in State Constitutions, would it not just as naturally, in the absence of any especial stress to the contrary, embody itself in the United States Constitution? And if any special stress prevented the recognition of its obligation in the one case, why would not a similar stress prevent it in the other? Besides, would not silence on this subject in the United States Constitution tend to produce a like silence in every other department of the Government? If its mention is unimportant here, can it be otherwise than unimportant anywhere? Important, or unimportant, the example of the National Congress may be expected to be potent throughout every subordinate department of the Government; just as our great cities, by their examples in things evil, as well as good, exert a controlling influence over the towns and villages.

Nearly a century has passed since this omission was made. It is not too early, therefore, to look for some of its results. Three generations of men educated under the Constitution can hardly fail to exhibit some of its ripening fruits.

In the first place, then, we may notice among the results of this silence, an entire perversion of its meaning. It was originally intended quietly to dispose of the difficulty presented in the great diversity of religious opinions in the country; to bridge them over, and give every sect of Christians an equal position before the law. It is now being interpreted as a rejection of them all. Intended as a toleration of error, it has come to be transformed into a rejection of the truth.

Nor is this a solitary instance in our history of a like transformation. At the time of the establishment of the Constitution, it seemed to be assumed that slavery as an institution must soon cease to exist upon our soil. It asked not for justification; it sought no enduring tenure of life. It only asked not to be violently thrust out. It begged that its foreign means of support, the slave trade, might not be suppressed before a given time. It anticipated its fate at no distant period from that glowing fire of liberty which had caused the revolution itself.

But when it had gotten the respite it sought, it began to cuddle itself in its nest. It drew to itself nutriment; it struck out right and left; it became an interest; it demanded the same consideration given to other interests; it talked of its rights, and finally claimed that all other rights, if need be, must stand aside. So long as there was a single foot of soil over which it might not drag its chain, and from which it might not eject the votaries of liberty, its rights were infringed. Hence, when the nation gave it bounds, and said, "no more slave territory," it unsheathed the sword and deluged the land with blood. From being tolerated as an evil, soon to disappear, it came to be a great interest imperatively demanding its rights.

So has it been with the silence of our national character in regard to the authority of the Christian religion. What was meant as a toleration of differences among Christians has come to be interpreted as a rejection of Christianity itself. The older of you will remember with what indignation you heard years ago that a diplomat to an Eastern Court, urging the concluding of a treaty with the United States, denied that we are a Christian nation—a denial we could not legally controvert.

Upon the vantage ground thus gained, the enemies of Christianity are pushing their warfare against it. They demand that our civil polity, from the highest to the lowest places of the Government, shall be brought into harmony with the Constitution—that all recognitions of Christianity, whether in law or usage, shall cease. These demands are stated in their full proportions, and without the slightest disguise, by one of the boldest, as he is one of the ablest, of the rejectors of Christ and his authority. They are summed up in the following nine particulars:

"1. We demand that churches and other ecclesiastical property shall no longer be exempted from just taxation."

"2. We demand that the employment of chaplains in Congress, in State Legislatures, in the navy and militia, and in prisons, asylums, and all other institutions supported by public money, shall be discontinued."

On the hypothesis that the silence of the Constitution is a rejection of Christianity, and that such rejection is proper, these demands are logical and just. Church property renders no service and should not be exempt from taxation. Chaplains lend no aid in the tempering of law or reforming the criminal, and should not therefore be supported by tax upon the people.

"3. We demand that all public appropriations for sectarian, educational and charitable institutions shall cease."

By "sectarian," he means probably any form of Christian institutions, &c.

"4. We demand that all religious services now sustained by the Government shall be abolished;" [whether they be free or not? What becomes of liberty of conscience on the part of officers of the Government?] "And especially that the use of the Bible in the public schools, whether ostensibly as a text-book or avowedly as a book of religious worship, shall be prohibited."

The spirit of this demand would also eliminate all mention of God from our text-books of science, and all Christian extracts from our reading books.

"5. We demand that the appointment by the President of the United States, or by the Governors of the various States, of all religious festivals and fasts shall wholly cease."

"6. We demand that the judicial oath in the courts and in all other departments of the Government shall be abolished, and that simple affirmation under the pains and penalties of perjury shall be established in its stead."

Affirmation is now permitted. Why impose it upon all to the exclusion of the oath? Is this an enhancement of liberty?

"7. We demand that all laws, directly or indirectly enforcing the observance of Sunday as the Sabbath, shall be repealed."

No more paying your notes on Saturday when they fall due on Sunday; no more closing your business places on Sunday; no more of Sunday stillness in the marts of trade; no more exemption of Sunday from common-school time by the authorities of public instruction; no more closing of theatres, lecture halls, art galleries and public libraries on Sunday with any reference to its uses as a day of Christian worship; and all this to secure harmony with the Constitution..

"8. We demand that all laws looking to the enforcement of 'Christian' morality shall be abrogated, and that all laws shall be conformed to the requirements of natural morality," [whatever that may mean], "equal rights, and impartial liberty."

When these demands shall have been secured, we shall have sunk again to the morality of Pagan times. The mercy which now tempers our criminal laws will have given place to the savageness of barbarian lands. Where then shall we look for those "equal rights," and that "impartial liberty" which never ripened except under a Christian sun?

"9. We demand that not only in the Constitutions of the United States and of the several States, but also in the practical administration of the same, no privilege or advantage shall be conceded to Christianity or any other special religion; that our entire political system shall be founded and administered on a purely secular basis; and that, whatever changes shall prove necessary to this end shall be consistently, unflinchingly, and promptly made."

That is, in short, we demand that this Government shall be "unflinchingly and promptly" reduced to the nihilism of Atheism. Rather a big job. And when accomplished, what next? Will it rest there? The human constitution makes man a religious being just as it makes him a social being. Eliminate the Christian religion, and you but clear the field for something else. Heathenism will take its place, and all the superstitions and corruptions of heathenism will abound.

The truth is, there can be no morality, natural or special, that has not God in it. All genuine moral laws have man at one end and God at the other. We have heard so much about development these later years, that not a few suppose that God has been developed *out* of the Universe, and morality developed *into* it; while the most conspicuous of all our modern developments is the egotism of boastful learning.

These being the modest demands of Liberalism, let us inquire how much it has really accomplished.

It has, as we have seen, demanded the elimination of all mention of God and Christianity from the State Constitutions in order to bring them into harmony with the United States Constitution. I have before me no data upon this subject; but from the nature of the problem I judge very little has been attained. The occasions for a modification of State Constitutions are few; and where they arise the appeal to a central board is inadequate, usually, to the end at which it aims.

In some other particulars its success has been more flattering. The Bible has been ejected from the public schools in various quarters and for various ostensible reasons, among which, strange to say, we sometimes find the very reverence in which it is professedly held—a reason akin to that which would exclude religion from politics, lest it should be contaminated. As the States move forward in the work of compulsory education, they will find themselves confronted with the grave alternative of teaching Christian morality as a part of that education, or of turning annually upon the community an increasing number of keen-sighted enemies of public order.

Another work in which the enemies of Christianity are meeting with some success is the opening of public libraries on Sunday. The significance of this measure is appreciated by relatively few. The reasons urged are plausible, and to a certain extent true; but they will commonly apply to art galleries, lecture halls, and even our public schools, with equal force. It is said, men and women had better loiter in public libraries than in the streets or drinking saloons. The same may be said of our children and the public schools. It is claimed that our libraries benefit the Sunday because they are public charities. In itself considered, were that the whole problem, men, women and children had better be found on Sunday in any of these places—public schools, lecture halls, art galleries, or even theatres, than in the grosser haunts of vice. But that is no part of the problem. To assume that they must be in the one class of places or the other is wholly gratuitous. The closing of the library does not necessitate the opening of the dram shop; and, if it did, it would still, possibly, be better that *some* persons should visit places of vice under their own and the public condemnation, than that the Sunday of quiet worship should be lost to the whole community. It becomes us well to consider whether the canting plea for the opening of our libraries is not the thin end of the wedge, whose full proportions are seen in the extraordinary demands above mentioned.

A philosopher, who detects the subtle influences which temper civil life and business honor, will be likely to conclude that a far deeper mischief than the foregoing has already been wrought by the assumption that our government rests on a purely *secular* basis, and ought to rest there. We know the engrossing and even debasing influence of secular affairs when one surrenders himself to them. Who of you has not, after a week of jading toil, come to your Sunday worship and found inspiration, renovation, and a nobler ambition for future endeavor? Better still has been the experience of those who have borne constantly in their souls a quickening sense of God's presence and authority. Things secular become sacred; and work becomes divine. Who can say to what extent we owe our recent great national scandal (Credit Mobilier) which mantles our cheek with shame and disgraces us in the eyes of the nations, to the prevailing secular theories of government? Who can say to what extent such influences operate to corrupt our politicians and poison the foundations of civil life?

Another pernicious result of the silence of our fundamental law in regard to Christianity is the inability of the Government consistently to deal with that foulest blot upon our modern civilization, the polygamy of Mormonism. Our President has recently indicated his purpose to take this matter in hand. Congress and the country appear to assent thereto. But with Christianity eliminated from every department of the Government, what warrant would there be for such proceedings? Do not Christianity and Mormonism stand on precisely equal grounds before our National Constitution? Must not Mormonism, if condemned at all, be condemned outside of the Constitution? Would not the philosophy we are opposing paralyze the nation in the direction of its noblest endeavors? Can there be freedom without law; and would not the elimination of Christianity, which is in reality our highest and our fundamental law, make noblest freedom impossible to us?

Is this the road our fathers intended to travel? Is it the road we, their sons, are willing to travel? Has this nation ever undertaken the dubious business of eliminating all differences of opinion? Does this noble theory of toleration even imply the opposite philosophy—the duty of suppressing, in all its laws and in the expression of its varied functions, whatever is in conflict with any man's conscience? Christianity infringes the Atheist's conscience no more than does Atheism the Christian's conscience. It is as far from his house to ours as it is from ours to his.

Recognize Christianity as our fundamental law, and we change this vantage ground. The recognition should, of course, be in fitting terms; not in terms that can be defended merely, but in terms that in their clearness and freedom from ambiguity need no defense. Such an amendment would work no miracle. By influence, not magic, would it bless the nation. It would furnish anchorage for the national faith; it would legitimate the influence of Christian morality in modifying criminal law; it would legitimate the spirit of Christianity in all law.

But it is said persecution will follow. How? It is not a union of Church and State. It is a recognition of no *church*, but of that which lies behind all churches—Christianity itself. It is proposed to base no legislation upon it; and it can, therefore, stretch out no hand to oppress any man or tyrannize over him. Most of our State Constitutions have similar provisions. These are much nearer to the people than the United States Constitution, and yet no tendencies to persecution have been exhibited. Educating influence, not restraining power, is the sole agency it could wield. That agency, from the high places of the nation, it would wield with power and efficiency. Whatever others may do, I wish to record my voice in its favor. When the serried ranks of infidelity shall demand the suppression of the name of God and of the mention of Christianity, I wish to stand among those who will say them Nay—among those who rejoice in the purpose, promise, efficiency, and glory of Christ's kingdom among men.

The Rev. Dr. Geo. P. Hays, President of Washington and Jefferson College, Pa., being introduced by the President, delivered the following address on the "Influence and Education of Public Sentiment:"

ADDRESS OF PRESIDENT HAYS.

It is true of other forms of government, but preëminently true of Republics, that no law can be enforced which is not supported by the sentiments of the people. Temperance legislation is good, but it has never been enforced against the wishes of the mass. Usury laws were thought to be good, and at one time were enforced with severe penalties, but so soon as the people came to look on the use of money as a commodity like wheat or iron, interest rose and fell like other prices, and usury laws became a dead letter on the statute book.

With this in mind, many are puzzled to understand why, when the sentiment of the revolutionary fathers was so unquestionably Christian, the fact does not show itself in the Constitution. But we shall not be surprised at this if we remember that they had been accustomed to the whole system of common law prevalent in England; and if we compare our constitutional history and the tendencies of our legal practice with that of England, we shall see that, while this amendment was not so essential then, it is now becoming increasingly important every day.

In England there is no written Constitution. Immemorial custom there is law, and is so enforced by the courts. Even the most important regulations of their administration of government are often unwritten. No written enactment ever declared, that, when a vote of want of confidence in the ministry passed the House of Commons, the ministry must either resign or appeal to the people by dissolving Parliament, and calling a new election. And yet should the British Queen and her ministry refuse to abide by that regulation, and submit to the voice of the people, so declared, a revolution would be precipitated as certainly as if the President here should undertake to perpetuate his power after his term had expired, and another had been elected to fill his place. A capital illustration of what is meant by common law is found in our war of 1812. Every one knows that the last war with England sprang up almost solely upon England's claim to the right to take American seamen from American vessels and impress them into the English service, because they had formerly been Englishmen. Over that question these two countries fought persistently and bravely. By-and-bye the ambassadors of the two nations met to make a treaty of peace, and in that treaty not one word is said of the impressment of seamen. No allusion to that subject, not even the most distant, can be detected. And yet that question was surely settled by the war, and finally settled. England has never tried to enforce impressment since, and, so far as I know, has never asserted the claim, and if to-day she was to try to enforce it, although we have no treaty stipulation to refer to in justification of our resistance, it would be resisted to the bitter end. It is common law between the nations.

Now, in England a very large part of their practice is common law practice, and in arguing it, all past historical facts are of the utmost importance; and in its decisions the courts will have high regard for the sentiments of the people, the public welfare, and past history. So in the beginning of the history of this country, English common law was common law here. A man was, I believe, once punished for gross blasphemy in New York under an indictment at common law. But the genius of our institutions has steadily drifted us away from common law practice to statute law. We began by having, first, Articles of Confederation, and then a written Constitution, in which it was distinctly provided that the powers not given to the Federal Government are reserved by the people; and then, to still further magnify statute law and diminish common law, we have Congress meeting in protracted annual sessions, legislating on all conceivable subjects, and discussing many inconceivable ones, and the State Legislatures racking their wits to find subjects whereon to legislate. Nothing but the dexterity of the criminal population can invent a subject not yet definitely mapped out, with its right and wrong all laid down in the law books. Go into the courts, and almost always in civil suits, and always in criminal suits, the prosecution opens his case by citing the law under which the suit is brought. You do know that here in New York are villains running unwhipped of justice because their crimes are not defined, with penalties attached, in the statute book. All the time our ignorant villains in the rural districts are swindled out of large sums of money, sent to bogus firms in New York for counterfeit National Bank notes, instead of which they only get sawdust; and when they come on here, they can do nothing in the New York courts, because the New York Legislature has not passed an act prohibiting lumber mills from furnishing sawdust for such purposes. (Laughter.) The President of our local Association was not long since on a jury, where the testimony proved that a farm was sold, and a large part of the purchase money paid. Shortly after the sale the seller died, and his widow married again before the deed was made out, when her second husband suggested that she had not, in full legal form, given her consent to the act of her first husband; and that jury, reluctant as they were, by the explicit charge of the court, were compelled to bring in a verdict by which that purchaser was required to pay the second time for what he had already paid. The justice and the right went for nothing when the letter of the law stood in the way. Just so now, it is capable of the most positive proof, on any platform, that Christianity was at the first, and ever since has been, an essential part of the political life of this nation; and if common law was the governing practice of this nation, the record of the past would be conclusive for the future, just so long as the churches kept up the religious sentiments of the citizens; but since more and more we are drifting away from common to statute law, what will all these avail in the presence of a specific enactment? In England the courts may condemn that which is against public morality, but here no moral evil can be a civil wrong until the Legislatures have passed upon it.

Driven thus by the very nature and genius of our American political institutions away from common law to specific legislation, we are compelled to have a standard fixed and settled, to which all can appeal, by which virtue and vice is to be tested. A criminal code is impossible without a standard, and there never was a more impossible fancy than laws, courts and penalties indifferent among deities. Jupiter justified wife murder and robbery; Moloch required the sacrifice of children; Boodh is pleased with the burning of widows; Joe Smith's Mormon god inculcates polygamy; the Mohammedans get from the harem to Heaven by the battle-field, as the shortest route; Compte, while scouting everything Christian in constructing his positive politics, deified collective humanity; and France, in her baldest atheism, worshipped a strumpet as the Goddess of Liberty; while Jehovah would have us do justly, love mercy and walk humbly. When now you deal with crimes and civil rights, you must decide among these. Non-committalism is impossible.

But some say there is no need of deciding, for the voice of the people is the law of the land. If that is true, polygamy is right in Utah; and a vote of the people and the Legislature can make it right to refuse to pay debts. Has the civil government the right thus to legalize fraud and cheating? We are now in a transition state in regard to the standard of weights and measures. It is to be hoped we shall soon come to use the decimal system there, as we now do in our money. Beyond doubt the law-makers can legislate the old cumbrous system out of existence, and the new in. Is the standard of crimes of the same character, so that it is only a matter of convenience whether crimes are voted up or down? Can the marriage tie and the sanctity of the household be thrust aside as pounds, shillings and pence have been ? We have come very near to that pass. We now ballot on the Sabbath question, and on the temperance question : why may we not with equal propriety vote on marriage? Sirs, ten millions of a majority would not make free-love and licentiousness right. We are drifting swift and sure to social chaos, whenever the popular sentiment adopts the principle that the right or wrong of moral questions may be readjusted at the ballot box.

But just here comes up the old cry, which, appealing to the sentiments of prejudice in the past, says this is uniting church and state, and on that four-fifths of the opposition of moral people to this movement depends. But we have shown that neutrality is impossible, if we are to have a criminal code at all, and as all experience proves the Bible and its moral law the best ever suggested to man, we have no rational alternative but to adopt it not only as the higher law, but the highest law of the land. Moreover, it is just as easy to mark out the proper boundaries of the province of the church, and the province of the state, with the Bible as without it. Indeed I do not believe it is possible to do it intelligently without the Bible. It never has been done without it. No nation ignorant of the Bible ever yet kept the two asunder. Whatever we know of the distinction between the two fields we gathered from inspiration. The most perfect specimen of spiritual despotism ever devised was that of Compte in his hostility to the Bible. Church and state both grope in the dark, as they search for their metes and bounds, when the light from heaven is gone. Whatever theory you may hold as to the field of the church and the state you can draw your dividing line with the Bible better than without it, or if not, it must be because the Bible contradicts your theory, and you had better abandon it. My theory is that the church was ordained of God to promote man's eternal welfare, and touches his temporal, only as it affects that, so that it is all the same to the church whether a man is a citizen or not—a president or a peasant—a millionaire or a beggar. On the other hand, the state was ordained of God to promote man's temporal welfare, and touches his eternal, only as it affects that, so that it is all the same to the state whether a man is a Jew or a Gentile—goes to heaven or to hell. These two fields are perfectly distinct, yet bear one upon another, and God and the Bible are as indispensable to the state in the oaths, crimes, punishments, and social virtue which affects man's temporal prosperity, as they are to the worship, sacraments, instruction and discipline of the church in its labor for man's eternal salvation. But whether you accept that theory or have another of your own, you can work out your own theory, if it is true, better with the Bible than without it ; and this movement contemplates no more union of church and state in the future than there has been in the past, but, simply, that as we can no longer rely on unwritten common law, but are driven to decide this question, that the Constitution and laws of this nation shall be as explicit on this subject as they are on others ; we are not forcing an issue, but the drift of our nation's history is forcing the issue on the nation.

It is wonderful how rapidly the issue is thrusting itself forward. Every ejectment of the Bible from the schools pushes it into prominence. Every anti-Sabbath mass meeting in Cincinnati attracts attention to it. Every riotous assault on the Orangemen in New York quickens the public sense of its urgency. Every categorical demand from the *Index* and the *Independent*, twin friends in a bad cause, compels those who would postpone it to see the impossibility of that; while the enormous debts plastered over New York by ring contractors, and the swindle of the Credit Mobilier in Washington, compels every honest man to see that not only must good morals be the sentiment of the people, but that the acknowledgment of God and obedience to the moral law must be explicitly required and rigidly enforced on those in high places; and give us but the same momentum of popular sentiment in this direction that rose against English impressment—that buried slavery beneath a constitutional amendment—and is coming slow, perhaps, but sure, on the temperance question—and for all the future forever it shall be settled in our Constitution and laws that Jehovah and His revelation is the standard of this nation's virtue, public and private.

How, then, shall such a public sentiment be developed? What means of education shall be adopted?

Among the measures of prime importance is a careful looking after the instruction given the young in our schools, academies, seminaries and colleges. Here are the men and women who are now acquiring that facility of tongue and felicity of expression which in years to come shall sway this nation. Here are the editors that from their sanctums shall send oracular utterances on rights and wrongs, to be received almost without question by their thousands of readers. Here are the lawyers that at the bar and on the bench shall expound justice to this nation. Here are the ministers that on these moral questions will be compelled, willing or unwilling, to deal with politics, and unless they are ready like cowards to abandon the commandments at the ominous shake of the partisan finger, they may have to fight a political battle to save the Sabbath. Here, too, especially, are the teachers, that in the public and private schools, higher and lower, will shape the sentiments of the people while yet they are in their bud and tender growth. The students of this land's colleges can mould the nation's doctrines in the next score of years, if they will. What is needed is that these students, while yet students, should know and appreciate the depth to which the beliefs they adopt will sink into the substratum of their emotional natures, and feel, therefore, the importance of making thorough work in their search for the right. This is just one reason why the reading of the Bible in our common schools is to be insisted upon. We are often asked, how much of what a child reads it remembers, rhyming it over without any thought or attention; and it is surely very doubtful if it remembers much, so as to say, "this and that moral truth I learned at school, reading the Bible." But we are not able to tell where and when, and how, we learned half of what we believe. The time of its absorption is not in our mind as a fact of consciousness, for the reason that it may have been an unconscious inference, drawn from facts, where even now the connection between the fact and the inference drawn would be scarcely perceptible to our more experienced observation. So the children now in our common schools are absorbing the faiths to which they will cling in after life with a tenacity far greater than that with which they will hold what they have seen proved in older years; and it is no mean method of educating their sentiments that every day they should take up this one Book solely because of its character and authority, and read it with that unexpressed but understood feeling that for some special reason this is the standard of right and wrong. If they never remember a sentence of its teachings at the time, but only know to turn to it as the test of the truth, *that* is an infinite gain. Added to this, however, there is that perpetual absorption of its spirit from parable, proverb, prophecy, miracle, sermon and history, which imprint indelibly on the mind and heart the beauty and safety of doing right, and the peril of doing wrong. Continue now the process through all the days of the months of the four or six school years of life, and those years of child-life, and it will be, wholly contrary to all other human experience of early impressions if the whole subsequent history is not mightily moulded by the education of conscience received therefrom. As the growing tree draws its substance not merely from the soil through which its roots run, seeking nourishment, but draws scarcely less from the atmosphere with which its leaves are surrounded, and the breezes that blow past it, so the young people of modern society learn not merely what they are sent to school to study, but are catching ideas and bents of mind from all their eyes see and ears hear by the way. Around their minds, too, there is an atmosphere that may be far more than one-fourth the soul-quickening oxygen of vigorous thought redolent with the aroma of Heaven, or hot with the blasphemous breath of hell. If this land is to be saved it must be largely done by controlling the influences that educate the sentiments of the young. Those in the anti-Sabbath movement have rightly begun their work by attempting the expulsion of the Bible from the schools, and as that is needful for them, so the preservation of that school Bible and such like influences is essential to the highest moral welfare of the nation.

But these judicious methods will not alone answer for the maintenance of right sentiments. Oftentimes the right bents that are received when young are lost as the individuals on entering society lose their individuality. Personal opinion is often over-slaughed and obliterated by the resistance or pressure of party power. In this land fashion controls the women, and political whips the men, and individual conscience and responsibility is lost in the mass. There are far too few men and women who do their own thinking. The majority dress as their circle dresses; sing the songs their set sings; vote the ticket their party nominates, and swear by the editorials of the newspaper that prints the flag of their fathers on its title-page. Under such circumstances it is easy to divide and sub-divide sin until each separate portion becomes so small that it is pushed aside as too insignificant to be much thought of. As a result, women have so much tortured and distorted their bodies and the laws of health, that it is seriously discussed whether we have a well woman in the land; and men have so degraded public office that it is denied that an honest man can be a politician; and every man that scratches his ticket is denounced as a renegade, and expelled from all parties. In the same way workingmen's associations prohibit tradesmen from working except at such prices as they may fix; and business men bind each other to sell at the same price, and ostracize the man that breaks the market. That social demoralization should result is as certain as any law of social science. Corruptions never come alone, just as no man ever falls suddenly into the commission of some enormous crime. Step by step the individual familiarizes his thoughts with crime, blunts his conscience and blinds his vision, until the first the public know a trusted citizen is revealed a corrupt scoundrel. So, one by one, corruptions come in, and we flatter ourselves that they are limited to a single sphere until some one inquires, and the difficulty is to find a clean spot.

The remedy is well begun when individual responsibility can be made the watchword of the nation, and independent action the practice of the people. Vice is already checked when men can be made to look down into their own eyes and recognize the guilt therein Will it be said that it is but little that a few can do in a task so extensive as this ? It needs but a determined few to take the lead. A hundred resolute men in either party in any county in the land can control their party, if they will scorn the party lash, and laugh in the face of the whipper. Vice is essentially, thoroughly, universally cowardly. There is not a brave man in your penitentiary. So in society, morality is far too sensitive to ridicule, but it is not half so sensitive as crime. He who thinks out his own right way and pursues it to the end, serves to stiffen the resolution of every half-minded man who is undecided in action.

When they say to us, " What good will this religious amendment do without the popular sentiment to back it ?" I answer I care nothing for the amendment if it was to be slipped quietly in as a matter of no importance. But this struggle for that amendment is the very best possible method of preserving the religious sentiment of the past and strengthening it for the future. Give us the right public sentiment and that amendment will go in with a whirl, *and that sentiment is indispensable to the perpetuity of the nation.* The amendment, without the popular sentiment corresponding, would be but a false profession of religion. The sentiment without the amendment would be the skulking Christian ashamed of, and denying his Master ; while the sentiment and the amendment is the nation rising up into a higher Christian life, and shining in the brightness of the King of the kingdoms of men.

The Convention then, at a late hour, adjourned to meet on the following morning at nine o'clock.

PROCEEDINGS OF THURSDAY, FEB. 27.

MORNING SESSION.

The Convention re-assembled at nine o'clock, and, in the absence of the President, was called to order by the First Vice-President, Jno. Alexander, Esq. At the invitation of the Chairman, Dr. J. Edwards led the Convention in prayer.

The President soon appeared and took the chair.

Many letters and other communications were sent to the Convention. Several remonstrances against the object of the Convention were referred to the Executive Committee. The number of friendly communications was too large to permit notice of them all. The following are selected as of special interest:

From the Hon. M. B. Hagans, Judge of the Superior Court of Cincinnati, and President of the last National Convention.

CINCINNATI, Feb. 18, 1873.

REV. D. MCALLISTER, New York.—*My Dear Sir* :—I received the call for the National Convention for securing the proposed Religious Amendment to the Constitution of the United States. The boldness of the enemies of this movement is, I am quite sure, arousing the careful attention of thoughtful and candid men all over the country. I am satisfied that our objects are misunderstood by a large body of both clergy and laity, and others are indifferent because they do not see the imminent danger we are in, with respect to the vital and fundamental principles that underlie the Government. I am glad to see this call; and to feel assured that the agitation of the question must result in success.

While I am sorry I cannot be present, I feel a deeper and more abiding interest in the movement. We need no more cogent arguments than those presented by the so-called "Liberals." But God will restrain the wrath of His enemies.

I wish the Convention all success, and pray the Divine Blessing on its sessions.

Very truly yours,

M. B. HAGANS.

From the Rev. Charles Hodge, D. D.

PRINCETON, Dec. 24, 1872.

REV. D. MCALLISTER:—I heartily approve of the object of the proposed meeting; but would greatly prefer that it was a call to secure the national acknowledgment of Christ as Him into whose hands all power in heaven and earth has been committed.*

CHARLES HODGE.

From Prof. Tayler Lewis, LL. D.

UNION COLLEGE, SCHENECTADY, Jan. 20, 1873.

MY DEAR FRIEND:—I have delayed answering you, partly from my poor health and incessant occupation, and partly from indecision. This has arisen from a desire to comply with your request, if I could. I am, however, convinced that I cannot prudently give you an affirmative answer. * * * * The great work in which you are engaged has my whole heart, and it gives me real regret to decline any part you may think fit to assign to me.

Yours truly,

TAYLER LEWIS.

From Prof. O. N. Stoddard, LL. D.

WOOSTER, O., Feb. 24, 1873.

REV. T. P. STEVENSON.—*Dear Friend*:—I regret very much that I cannot attend the Convention in New York. I could not, consistently with my duties to the University, be absent during the time necessary for the trip and attendance on the Convention.

I have never faltered for a moment in my interest for this cause. It is not specially for Christianity that I have rendered what little aid I could. Christianity can live without the amendment; the nation cannot. Patriotism, were there nothing higher, would require that our Government should be put *officially in its true relation to God. The nation does not treat God with the respect which one gentleman would observe towards another, so long as it refuses to recognize Him in that Constitution which, in form, sets forth the principles on which the nation's character is based, and by which it must be judged in the court of Heaven.*

We are seeking the highest interests of the men who oppose. I trust your deliberations will be guided with the wisdom and prudence which the Spirit bestows.

With kind regards,

Yours truly,

O. N. STODDARD.

---

* Dr. Hodge's attention was subsequently called to the fact that the National Association labors to secure such an amendment as will suitably recognize Christ as the Ruler of nations, when he remarked, "I had overlooked that. That is satisfactory."

From the Students of Dane Law School, Harvard University.

CAMBRIDGE, Mass., Feb. 22d, 1873.

D. MCALLISTER, *Gen. Sec.—Dear Sir:*—We enclose minutes of the action taken by the "Assembly of Harvard Law School" in regard to the call for a National Convention to secure a religous amendment to the Constitution of the United States.

Our duties at the University prevent our attendance in person at the Convention called to meet in New York on Wednesday, the 26th inst.

With heartfelt sympathy for the success of this movement, we remain, very truly,

F. W. EDGAR, *Easton, Penn.*
JAS. C. BERGEN, *Brooklyn, New York.*
JAS. R. RIGGINS, *Kansas City, Mo.*

CAMBRIDGE, Feb. 22d, 1873.

At a regular meeting of the "Assembly of Dane Law School" of Harvard University, held Friday evening, 21st February, 1873, it was *voted*, That a committee of three be appointed to serve as delegates to represent this assembly in New York, on next Wednesday, for the purpose of considering a religious amendment to the Constitution. *Voted*, That Messrs. Edgar, Bergen and Riggins be appointed such a committee.

LEWIS C. LEDYARD, *Clerk.*
D. D. BURNES, *Speaker.*

A letter of peculiar interest, expressive of the transatlantic interest and sympathy referred to in the Report of the Secretary, is the following:

From the Rev. Dr. James Begg, Edinburgh.

50 GEORGE SQUARE, EDINBURGH, Feb. 3, 1873.

MY DEAR SIR:—Perhaps you will allow a minister of the Free Church of Scotland to express his great satisfaction in connection with your noble effort to amend the Constitution of the United States. I can imagine no higher manifestation of patriotism, and I earnestly trust and pray that your efforts may be crowned with complete success. I read with much interest and satisfaction the CHRISTIAN STATESMEN, which some kind friend is good enough to send, and, if it were possible, I should have the greatest satisfaction in attending your meeting on the 26th. I hope to have an opportunity of reading an account of its proceedings, and of giving some information to many in Scotland, who are beginning to look on with interest. We have here, in several forms, a struggle going on for substantially the same principles for which you are contending; principles which must ultimately be crowned with triumphant success. Wishing you all prosperity and blessing in your noble work, I am, my dear sir, yours, very faithfully,

JAMES BEGG.

To the General Secretary, etc.

The Resolutions reported at last evening's session were taken up and discussed *seriatim* for adoption. After considerable animated discussion, and some slight amendments, the Resolutions were adopted.* They are as follows:

* It was intended to give in full this discussion, in which Messrs. Edwards, Sloane, J. C. K. Milligan, Collins, Wardell, Crozier, Mrs. J. G. Swisshelm, and others, took part, as reported by the Rev. W. H. Tiffany, the stenographer of the Convention. But the limits within which it has been judged best to confine this volume will not permit the carrying out of the original intention. Prepared addresses and reports occupy much space, and in their fullness render unnecessary anything more than a running account of other matters.

RESOLUTIONS.

Resolved, 1. That this Ninth General Convention of the National Association for the Religious Amendment of the Constitution of the United States re-affirms its deep conviction of the greatness and the necessity of the work in which it is engaged.

Resolved, 2. That the principles which underlie this movement commend themselves to the common sense and the conscience of men as true, as practical, and as of great importance.

Resolved, 3. That, in the judgment of this Convention, a nation and an administration of government can no more exist without moral character, moral influence and religion, than without a language, and that any attempt to do so is not only absurd but dangerous.

Resolved, 4. That it is the clear right and duty of a Christian people to make in their national Constitution solemn acknowledgment of God as the author of government, and to make unmistakable mention of their preference of Christianity as their religion, both that God may thus be duly honored, and that legal presumptions may be created in favor of Christian morality, Christian usages, and Christian institutions.

Resolved, 5. That such acknowledgment of God and of Revelation is not designed, and does not tend in any wise, to oppress any individual conscience, or to effect any union of Church and State, nor can it ever be pleaded, used, or even perverted, to such injurious ends.

Resolved, 6. That this Convention does not regard as at all essential the precise form of petition sent to Congress in the interests of this Reform, provided the main issue be fairly included, viz., that it is impossible for a State to be neutral in religion and morals; and that the Christian religion is an essential element in American civilization, as shown in the whole history of this country.

Resolved, 7. That the signs of the times, the rapid deterioration of public morals, and the bold demands of organized political infidelity, show conclusively and impressively, that the alternative now presented to the American people is Atheism or Christianity, and that failure to adopt this proposed amendment involves ultimately general immorality and anarchy.

Resolved, 8. That, thanking God and taking courage upon a review of the past, this Convention declares the time to be fully come for more extended agencies than have heretofore been employed, and that especially it is important to secure systematic and liberal contribution of funds for this purpose.

The General Secretary of the National Association next presented his report, which was adopted and ordered to be published with the proceedings of the Convention. It is as follows:

GENERAL SECRETARY'S REPORT.

The progress of the movement for the Religious Amendment of the Constitution of the United States, during the past year, has far exceeded the expectations of its most sanguine friends.

The Convention held last year in Cincinnati called public attention to the movement more fully and pointedly than ever before, and created a wide demand for information. For the rapidly-increasing friends of the cause a frequent medium of communication was required, and the reports of meetings were constantly demanding a hearing.

To meet these and other similar demands a weekly paper became indispensably necessary. Accordingly, considerable time was spent soon after the Cincinnati Convention in securing the formation of an association for the publication of a weekly journal. The effort met with such success that, on the first of last September, the CHRISTIAN STATESMAN, the organ of this movement, was issued as a weekly, a neat eight-page journal, in quarto form, and on a good financial basis. The experience of the past six months abundantly proves the stability of this enterprise, and its invaluable aid in the prosecution of our work.

The need was also felt for other documents, presenting fuller treatment of certain aspects of the question than could find place in a single number of the paper, and in shape for preservation. To supply this want the proceedings of the last Convention were published in a pamphlet of about ninety pages, containing an account of the origin and progress of the movement, and the addresses of Judge Hagans, Dr. A. D. Mayo, Profs. Tayler Lewis, Stoddard and Sloane, and others. This valuable pamphlet has been circulated widely over our own country, going into the hands of thoughtful, leading men, and not a few copies have been applied for from beyond the Atlantic. A sixteen-page tract on the Bible in the Public Schools, the third of the series of CHRISTIAN STATESMAN tracts, has also been published, and several thousands of copies distributed, particularly through the State of New York. Many thousands of other and familiar documents have also been distributed.

It is impossible to give an accurate statement of the number of meetings held in the interest of this cause during the past year. Information has been received of several hundreds of public meetings at which earnest addresses have been delivered. Judges, lawyers, professors, and ministers have been among the speakers. This stirring gathering of several hundreds of delegates from nineteen States is itself proof of the large number of meetings held. Many letters have been received, expressing sympathy, and conveying to this Convention resolutions passed at meetings from which no delegates have come.

Though there have been several times as many public meetings as ever before, for the same period, during the past year, little has been done in organizing local auxiliary societies. From fifteen to twenty of these have been formed, within the past twelve months, in the following States, viz.: Massachusetts, New York, Pennsylvania, Ohio, Indiana, Iowa, and Kansas. One of these societies, formed in St. Lawrence County, N. Y., has already, in a few months, enrolled three hundred and seventy-five members.

The effects of the year's work are most distinctly marked. Among them I would call attention to the following:

The whole subject of the relation of civil government to Christianity is now receiving wide and careful attention. It is being discussed not only in the newspapers, but in ministers' meetings, in colleges, lyceums, and in an increasing number of pamphlets and books. The Western Tract and Book Society of Cincinnati have recently offered an award of $100 for the best discussion of the relation of the United States Government to Christianity, and the duty of expressing that relation in the fundamental law. The same subject is to be carefully discussed at the meeting of the Evangelical Alliance in this city next Fall.

Again, the issue has become more clearly defined. The aggressive action of the enemies of the Christian institutions of the nation is dissipating the fogs of misapprehension. Thousands who have heretofore questioned the expediency of the Religious Amendment movement have been led to revise their opinion.

Accordingly, from all quarters, during the work of preparation for this

Convention, tidings kept pouring in of earnest and active friends coming to the front. The names attached to the call for the Convention, representing as they do all portions of our land,—from Maine to California, and from the Lakes to the Gulf,—indicate the marvelous growth of this movement during the past twelve months. As an able Methodist minister said at a meeting in one of the principal cities of New Jersey, "It needs only to be fairly presented before the Christian people of the country, and it will go like an avalanche!" It is safe to say that it has far more than doubled its proportions within the year.

Another interesting and encouraging point to be noted is the warm expression of sympathy which comes from beyond the sea. As with us, there is in the most advanced Christian nations of Europe a strong party in favor of secularism. This party in Great Britain is striving to strip the Government of every Christian feature. Many of the warmest friends of Christian institutions favor disestablishment. But with them are many of the same stripe as those who are our legitimate opponents here—the enemies of the Christian religion. These are warring not only against the church establishments of Great Britain, but against every Christian element in the noblest institutions of that noble nation. The friends of Christian government there see that the question of the day with us, as well as with them, is the question of the relation of the state to religion. And well aware that Christians of all denominations here, opposed now, as they always have been, to the establishment and endowment of any church by the state, still unite in the endeavor to have our nation acknowledge God and Christ and the Bible, for itself in its own independent sphere, and not through the medium of any ecclesiastical establishment, our Christian brethren from across the Atlantic send us the expression of their most cordial sympathy, and the assurance of their prayers for our success.

In the present stage of the movement there is a manifest necessity for instant attention to the following points:

1. The friends of our Christian institutions should take measures at once for the most effective action and coöperation. They must organize. Wherever even a few of them are found they should form themselves into a society, and link themselves with the National Association.

2. To give enduring vitality to these organizations scattered through the country, a common work must be taken in hand. No more suitable work presents itself than the circulation of petitions. If this Convention should direct that petitions be prepared and placed in the hands of every local society, and if the members of this Convention, on their return home, in case a local organization has not yet been effected, should at once organize, and begin to hold meetings and secure signatures to the petition, we might send from the next National Convention a delegation to Congress, with hundreds of thousands of names praying for the desired amendment. Who can estimate what even one year's earnest work on the part of all of us might do?

3. To help forward the work of organization and of obtaining signatures to the petitions, as many lecturers as possible should take the field during all the fine weather of autumn, and for at least two months before the next National Convention.

4. To accomplish all this we must give liberally of our substance. We must live up to the words of an eloquent Baptist clergyman of a neighboring city,

who stirred the heart of the citizens at a large meeting there a few evenings since : "For my part, I am to be counted on the side of this cause in body, soul, time, influence, and pocket-book."

Allow me, in concluding this report, to suggest that members of this Convention be appointed to present the claims of the movement before the various bodies that may assemble during the year. I would also suggest that many of our number may help the cause in an effective way by preparing a report of the Convention for one of the religious weeklies, or for any local paper.

Fellow-laborers, let us pledge ourselves to-day, with prayer for Divine guidance, to renewed and more earnest efforts during the year before us.

The Executive Committee of the National Association next presented their report for the past year. The report was accepted, and its recommendations adopted. It is as follows :

REPORT OF THE EXECUTIVE COMMITTEE.

Your Committee would respectfully report :

1. That two thousand copies of the Proceedings of the National Convention at Cincinnati were published in pamphlet form, and judiciously distributed. An account of the origin and progress of the movement was prefixed to this report, and the whole pamphlet has been found of great service, as the most complete and comprehensive presentation of our principles and aims.

2. The report of the Treasurer herewith submitted, shows receipts during the year of $4,046.93, all of which has been acknowledged in the columns of the CHRISTIAN STATESMAN, and expenditures to the amount of $4,002.10, under the direction of your Committee, leaving a balance at date of $44.83.

3. The work has been rewarded during the year with the most gratifying success. More general information of the character of the Amendment which is proposed, and the increasing boldness and activity of the enemies of our Christian institutions, have led hundreds of thoughtful men heartily to espouse our cause ; and an earnest sympathy has been awakened in Great Britain, where the same principles are involved in a kindred struggle on the question of religious education.

4. Your Committee recommend the general circulation, during the next year, of petitions to Congress in behalf of the Amendment which we seek, and submit the following form for the adoption of this Convention :

To the Honorable, the Members of the Senate and House of Representatives, in Congress assembled :

The undersigned, citizens of the United States, petition your honorable bodies for such an amendment to the Constitution of the United States, as will suitably express our national acknowledgment of Almighty God as the source of all authority in civil government, of the Lord Jesus Christ as the Ruler of nations, and of His revealed will as of supreme authority ; and thus indicate that this is a Christian nation, and place all the Christian laws, institutions and usages of the Government on an undeniable legal basis in the fundamental law of the land.

5. Your Committee recommend that this Convention do, and hereby does, respectfully request the Constitutional Convention of Pennsylvania, now in session in the City of Philadelphia, to place suitable religious acknowledgments in the draft of the Constitution to be submitted to the people of that State for their adoption, and that the delegates from Pennsylvania in this

Convention be appointed to bear this request to that body. We recommend, further, that the Executive Committee to be appointed at this Convention be charged to present a similar request on behalf of the National Association to the Constitutional Convention of Ohio, and to other similar Conventions which may meet during the year,

6. Your Committee recommend that a subscription be taken up in this Convention for the treasury of the National Associatión.

7. That the delegates to this Convention be recommended to hold meetings in their several localities, to ratify its proceedings, and to form, wherever practicable, societies auxiliary to the National Association.

A resolution presented by Mrs. JANE G. SWISSHELM was referred to the Committee on Resolutions, and, after slight modification, was adopted in the following form:

Resolved, That the cause for which this Convention has met is one that commends itself to the special sympathy and concern of the Christian women of our land, and they are confidently relied upon for their earnest coöperation in giving it final success.

This resolution called forth an animated discussion, in which there was a hearty recognition of the importance of woman's aid in every good work.

On motion, the Convention adjourned to meet at two o'clock P. M.

AFTERNOON SESSION.

The Convention was called to order by the First Vice-President, Mr. John Alexander, who called on the Rev. Dr. Sloane to open the meeting with prayer.

After the transaction of unimportant business, the President appeared, took the chair, and introduced the Rev. J. P. Lytle, of Ohio, who spoke as follows:

ADDRESS OF MR. LYTLE.

MR. CHAIRMAN, AND GENTLEMEN OF THE CONVENTION: We meet in this place to advocate the adoption of what may be called the "17th Amendment to the Constitution of the United States," or, as it is usually called, "The Religious Amendment of the United States Constitution." The time was when the Constitution of the United States was regarded as so sacred an instrument, that to speak of amending it, or touching it in any form for the purpose of alteration, would have been regarded as sacrilege. But that time has, in the Providence of God, passed by. In our day, within ten years past, we have seen the Constitution of the United States amended, and amended, again and again; and the idea that it, as first formed, contained the perfection of all human wisdom, has been dissipated, and we have come to discover that it was a delusion. We have already passed upon, and adopted the 14th and the 15th, and likewise the 16th Amendment. We have through that document abolished slavery wherever the Stars and Stripes float. We have, by the same process, made all men of all colors, and of all nations, equal before the law, and we have established universal suffrage. Now, then, having thus secured and guaranteed by the Constitution the rights of man, we seek to go still further, and in this grand instrument which commands the respect of not only the citizens of the United States, but of all the world, we seek to secure the acknowledgment of Almighty God, the author and preserver of our national existence. And in doing so, we are not ignorant of the fact that we shall encounter formidable opposition. Everywhere clouds dark and lowering gather in opposition to this movement. You have heard the muttering of the thunder of that infidel organ located at Toledo. You have heard the echo of this from the office of the *Independent*, even from the Senate of the United States. The Chairman of the Judiciary Committee, Mr. Trumbull, has said that "The Constitution of the United States needs no such amendment," and we have heard the response from the throne above, "And I have no need of you." [Applause.] The enemies of our movement naturally draw into their ranks all infidels, Jews, Jesuits, and all opposers of Him who is Lord over all, our Lord Jesus Christ.

It may be asked, "How shall we succeed against such a mighty host?" We are like Israel of old—"two little flocks of kids, while the Syrians fill the country." We are few, while our enemies fill the land. We look for success to two sources: first, we look up to that personal God, whose crown rights and royal prerogatives are involved in this question. [Applause.] And through Him "one shall chase a thousand, and two put ten thousand to flight." One with God at his side and God at his back is more than all the hosts of His enemies. We look to this mighty God who reigns over all for light, strength and success. Through Him we shall vanquish those who oppose us. That is not all: we look to another source.

We make very little account of ourselves in this contest. We look to others. We look to our enemies—to such men as speak through the *Index*—for powerful aid. The editor of that journal, far-sighted and frank, has seen and declared the state of things at which they aim, and the end which will have been accomplished when their principles have become popular. When the people see what these men hope and labor for, they will be shocked. Out in Ohio, at one point on the Baltimore and Ohio Railroad, on what is called "section 16," there is a very heavy grade. The locomotive, in attempting to ascend that grade, often sticks and stops, and the train rolls backward. To overcome this difficulty, they have what is called there a "helper"—a powerful engine to assist; and with this one pushing at the rear of the train and heading in the contrary direction, and the other engine pulling, the train is drawn up the hill. A stranger at a distance, looking at the train, with its engines pointed in opposite directions, would naturally suppose they would neutralize each other, pulling different ways. And if you stood at this end of the train, you might think the "helper" was about to run over you, and take the whole train with it. On examination, you would see that the machinery was really working in the other direction—actually pushing the train up the hill. Now, my friends, the train is the thirty-six or thirty-seven States of the Union. The section on which the difficulty connected with our cause occurs is not exactly "section 16," but it is section 17, in which we seek to have the amendment of the United States Constitution. And on this section the engine in front of the train is the Christian Association; and the other engine is Mr. Francis E. Abbot and Company in the *Index* and similar papers. Some think they are very dangerous, and will drag us all down into an abyss of infidelity, atheism, profligacy and ruin; but if you come a little closer and examine, you will see that their machinery is really working in the other direction.

We need something to arouse public sentiment; to reach the commercial classes and formal Christians; to show the American people at large the end aimed at by the advocates of the secular theory of government, as illustrated in the French Revolution of 1798, and the more recent Paris Commune. And what instrumentality could be better adapted to our work? The Christian Association enlisting friends by reason and argument, and the *Index* Association driving neutrals and indifferentists into the movement from sheer necessity of self-preservation; our enemies pushing and we pulling, and the power of God working over all, our onward course is certain. And when we reach the summit, Mr. Abbot and his "Helper" will be switched off the track; while the train will move out into the mild yet glorious light of Millennial days, and the cry will be raised, "The kingdoms of this world have become the kingdoms of our Lord, and of His Christ." [Applause.]

The President next introduced the Rev. John Hogg, of Massachusetts, who delivered the following address:

ADDRESS OF REV. J. HOGG.

Mr. President, Ladies and Gentlemen: When I listened to the magnificent addresses delivered here yesterday, I had no expectation of appearing on this platform. I feel that it is little short of presumption for me to stand here, and I do so merely to show what side I am on. [Applause.] You know that it takes all kinds of people to make a world, and all kinds of speakers to make up a convention. I remember reading once an anecdote of Coleridge, who, with all his genius, was in some things very awkward. Coming along a country road one day, riding on horseback with his knees almost up to his chin, he was met by a wag, who not knowing his man, and thinking to have a little fun, exclaimed: "Halloo, my man, did you meet a tailor on the way?" "Yes, sir," replied the wit, "and he told me that if I went a little further on I would meet a goose." And so it seems to me, that the eloquent speakers by whom I have been preceded, like scientific tailors, have been putting in their stitch, stitch, stitch, in the garments of glory and beauty with which we seek to clothe the nation, and now I am ready to be a goose, or anything else, to smooth down the seam. [Laughter and applause.]

I stand here to-day the representative of a large class of individuals, who might aptly be called the weak-backed and feeble-kneed. The truth is, I have been on the fence, uncertain on which side to get down. It is but lately that I have been led to examine the matter, feeling that the time has come when every honest man must take his position. [Applause.] I feel already the effect of being present at this Convention, for my back has been stiffened, and my heart strengthened for the work.

I have reached a conclusion in harmony with the object of this Convention, by something like the following process of thought: Starting with the idea that a nation is a moral entity, responsible to God for its actions, history seems to be little more than a record of the death of nations. The old empires of antiquity, about which so many volumes have been written, have passed away.

Even Rome itself, the grand old iron empire, had its decline and fall. And why? Some tell us that nations, like men, must necessarily, after full development, sink into dissolution. Others say that nations, when they enjoy prosperity and acquire wealth, become luxurious, immoral, and effeminate; and therein lie the seeds of death. It seems to me, however, that a nation's life depends wholly upon the character of its religion. Rome had religion enough to give her grit and energy for a time. Even Paganism could carry a nation a certain length, and still preserve a balance between the intellect and the conscience. So long as this was the case, Rome stood, and swayed a mighty sceptre; but when the intellect got in advance of her religion and repudiated it, then Rome went down. [Applause.] The only religion that can forever bind together and preserve a nation's life is the religion of the Lord Jesus Christ. The ideas of Jesus are ever in advance of human progress, and the most cultivated intellect acknowledges their power. Jesus said, "Whosoever believeth in me shall never die;" and what is true of an individual is also true of a nation. The nation that takes hold upon God and the Lord Jesus Christ shall never die. [Applause.]

That these United States are, on the whole, Christian, cannot be doubted. There are at least twenty-five millions of nominal Christians in our land. Is this Christianity to be made so operative as to secure our national life? The question is a momentous one. Is our nation to live or die? You heard a man hissing here yesterday. What is he? Just the representative of the vast mass of irreligion in our land. Perched on the summit of liberty, sacred only to holy purposes, and purchased by the blood of Christian martyrs, the hisses of the irreligious at every movement that would limit their abuse of liberty, sound the watchword of increased licentiousness, the death-knell of our nation's life. [Applause.] Again, the corruption at present existing in our land is appalling. The nation's conscience seems to be uncontrolled by its Christianity. There are breakers ahead, and unless the ship be turned on a different track I see no alternative but that she must founder. Our nation is but new born. Her first centennial has not yet been celebrated. Designed, doubtless, to work out some grand purpose of Divine Providence; born of Christian principles, and enjoying a birthright of Christian freedom, yet the Father of Nations is not acknowledged, and I fear His great name was designedly omitted from her organic law. I cannot agree altogether with some things said by preceding speakers, in their endeavor to account for this fatal defect. There is no connection between the establishment of a State religion, or minding the conscience of sectarians, and the acknowledgment of God as the Father of Nations. Infidelity, and nothing else, was the animus of the omission—the infidelity of Paine and of France with which some of the prominent framers of the Constitution were deeply imbued. If anything is needed to prove this position, it is found in the fact that they almost unanimously refused to ask Almighty God to guide them in their deliberations. I am apprehensive that our national Constitution, wisely framed though it be, is a child of merely human parents, and unless the defect be remedied, it must, like its authors, die. If we mean it to live, we must have it imbued with a divine life.

But it is said—"If the nation be on the whole Christian, what difference can an amendment of the Constitution make? Until lately this was to me a stumbling block. It appeared to me an act of mere formality. If done tomorrow it would not change the nation's character in the least degree. So I thought until reflection removed the difficulty. The lapse of a few score of years has not obliterated from the mind of God the fact, that the framers of the Constitution deliberately insulted Him, and that the whole people became implicated in that act. The fearful ordeal through which our nation has already passed, and the seething corruption which now fills us with foreboding fears, are but the fitting sequence of a nation's disregard of God. I can see no remedy but repentance—national repentance. If we expect God to honor us we must honor Him. We should confess and forsake our sins, and declare that we will give God His place as head of our nation. When we do this, then God will cause His face to shine upon us; but if we refuse, we can only expect the rod to fall upon us with increasing weight. You remember the period in our late civil war when the heart of the nation was crushed by continued reverses. A dark pall seemed to rest over a loyal people, and many were beginning to exclaim, "Give us peace and let the rebels go." It was then our lamented, martyred President performed one of the sublimest acts that history records. Taught of God, and no doubt grasping the idea that the chastising rod was in God's hand, he issued his Proclamation which broke the fetters from the slave. He drew his pen across that foul blot on the escutcheon of our nation. It was seemingly a formal thing. The Constitution legally fostered slavery. The President wiped the ugly thing out. The people shouted Amen! Slavery was abolished. Then mark the issue—victory at once perched on our banners. Our armies went forth conquering, until rebellion was finally subdued. Let us act similarly in respect to the remaining blot of Atheistic silence in the Constitution, and see if the tide of battle will not turn as evidently in favor of truth, righteousness and prosperity. Let us acknowledge God as our Father, and sovereign, and source of all good, and His blessing will be upon us. Crime and corruption will come to an end, and the benign reign of Jesus, our rightful Lord, will be established. [Applause.]

The Executive Committee reported in favor of granting twenty minutes to the opponents of the movement, who had sought opportunity to present their remonstrance and objections. This recommendation being approved by the Convention, the Chairman of the meeting at Vineland, N. J., appointed by some of the citizens of that place to appear before the Convention and protest against its object, took the platform. He was courteously and patiently heard, and the time allotted him was even extended, until a grossly disrespectful allusion to the Bible provoked indignant remonstrance from several members; and the permission accorded was withdrawn.

The Committee on Enrollment reported that 470 persons had enrolled themselves as members of the Convention, representing nineteen States and one Territory, and that three hundred and sixty-three bore certificates of their appointment as delegates by various public assemblies and organized societies.

The subscription recommended by the Committee on Resolutions, and by the Executive Committee, was then entered upon. The General Secretary stated that he had already received many and generous contributions from earnest friends who could not be present at the Convention, and after stating a number of instances of commendable liberality, read the following paper which had been placed in his hands:

By the Grace and Providence of God enabling me, I will contribute to the Treasury of the National Association for securing the amendment of the Constitution of the United States, the sum of *five hundred dollars*, annually, *until an amendment (in substance such as at present proposed by this Association) shall be made to the Constitution of the United States.*

If this amendment is not made during my lifetime, I shall hope to continue the aforesaid annual payments through the agency of the legal representatives of my estate.

"I can do all things through Christ which strengtheneth me."

Philadelphia, Feb. 26th, 1873.

JOHN ALEXANDER.

The impression produced by the calm and devout earnestness of this paper was deepened by the stirring speech of Walter T. Miller, Esq., of New York, who named twenty thousand dollars as the amount which can, and ought to be, raised this year for the work of the National Association, and who pledged himself to give the twentieth part of all the receipts of the treasury for the year.

Mr. Miller and Mr. James Wiggins, of New York, each subscribed $500, the latter also promising to give one-twentieth of $20,000. Henry Martin, Esq., and lady, of Cincinnati, subscribed $300; Dr. Magee, of White Ash, Pa., one-third of $1,000, the other two-thirds of which are to be given by Messrs. David Torrens, Jno. McWilliams, and some other liberal gentleman whose name we have not before us. We might go on and give the names of friends who this year, as heretofore, have given $100. But enough has been said to show how generously the response was made to the call for funds for an expansion of the work.

It is but due to Mr. Alexander, whose contribution of $500 is to be continued annually until the movement is crowned with success, to state that for this year, in addition to the five hundred dollars, he has most generously agreed to give $1,000, if by this additional contribution the whole sum for the year can be raised to $20,000.

The amount subscribed, apart from all sums promised conditionally, was $5,360.00. The receipts of the Association, from ordinary sources, will no doubt be larger this year than ever before. The National Association thus has placed at its disposal, for this year, two to three times as much as it has ever heretofore employed in its operations for a single year.

The President then introduced the Rev. H. H. George, President of the Geneva Collegiate Institute, Ohio, who spoke as follows:

ADDRESS BY PRESIDENT H. H. GEORGE.

The question of education is one that is fundamental to the interests and prosperity of any nation. To one, especially, whose government is by the people, it must be prejudicial to misconceive the importance of it, and only suicidal to ignore it. It requires no far-sightedness to perceive that as the youth of a country are educated, as their intellects are cultivated, and their moral natures are bent, such must sooner or later be the cast of the institutions of that country. Give me the vast multitudes of children in this land to control and educate as I will; let me prescribe the system of rules by which they shall be trained, furnish teacher and text-book, and I care not what your institutions are to-day, I will give such as suit myself before the lapse of many years.

If any man or party of men had it in purpose to revolutionize the government of a country, no more favorable point of attack, no more hopeful starting place, could be selected than the youth of that land in their first and most susceptible years of training. A great orator of this country has said: "The man who sets an idea on two feet, and bids it travel from Maine to Georgia, has done more to revolutionize his country than if, to overthrow the Capitol, he had put powder under the Senate chambers." And where can that molding, revolutionizing idea be more certainly and successfully started, than in the minds of the children as they learn their first lessons at the common schools?

The keen-sighted enemy of the Bible who hates the religion it inculcates, has fully comprehended this truth, and hence his first and furious attack is upon that Bible in the hands of the little boys and girls of our land just as they are learning to read. Well he knows the power of the leverage of the youthful mind, in his attempts to put down the Bible and secularize the institutions of the country.

But let us notice the prominence given to the moral and religious features of state education upon the page of history:

"*Religionibus et artibus sacrum*" has been written on the portals of schools, academies and colleges from time immemorial.

The schools of the ancient Grecian philosophers were devoted mainly to the study of the nature of the gods, and the spiritual nature of man.

Pythagoras taught the harmony of the universe, man's immortal destiny, and the paramount importance of his moral nature.

Aristotle taught to the Athenian youth a philosophy in which theology bore a most conspicuous place.

Trace the historic page from the Christian era, and we find religious teaching a predominating element in almost every century, and at no time was it considered less important than secular instruction.

Recognizing the fundamental importance of education, and especially its moral and religious character, those modern nations that have led the van of civilization and improvement have given it a distinct prominence in their systems of government.

In Dr. Stowe's report, a few years ago, to the Ohio Legislature, he says:

"In Germany the school system embraces a course of eight years, making four divisions of two years each." And after summing up the branches taught in these respective divisions, he adds: "In the first is given religious instruction and the singing of hymns; in the second is religious instruction in select Bible narratives; in the third is religious instruction in the connected Bible history; in the fourth division, including children from ten to sixteen years old, is given religious instruction on the religious observation of nature, the life and discourses of Jesus Christ, the history of the Christian religion in connection with the contemporary civil history, the doctrines of Christianity."

Barnard, in treating of the subjects and methods of instruction in Prussia, says: "That every complete elementary school in that country gives instruction in religion and morality, established on the positive truths of Christianity."

"In the public schools of Berlin instruction is given in the Bible, the Catechism, the positive truths of Christianity."

"In Switzerland a teacher must have a certificate from the clergyman of his own church that he is fitted, both by character and education, to conduct the religious instruction in the school for which he is designed."

"In Russia it is assumed that religious teaching constitutes the only solid foundation of all useful instruction."

Following the example of those olden nations, and learning a lesson from the pages of history, almost every State in our Union has made salutary laws concerning both the matter and the manner of the education of its youth. Let the constitutional provision of the noble State of Ohio suffice for illustration here:

"Religion, morality and knowledge being essentially necessary to good government and the happiness of mankind, schools and the means of instruction shall forever be encouraged by legislative provision not inconsistent with the rights of conscience."

Based upon this and similar provisions in the various State Constitutions, the public school has become one of our grandest and noblest institutions. Its influence for good has simply been incalculable. It has contributed largely to the moulding of our civilization, and has done much to elevate us to that honorable position we occupy among the nations of the world. Nor has it been hindered in its noble services, save only as the modern philosopher has come forward to call its founders fools and madmen, and to startle the world with a new light and a more liberal philosophy.

But let us inquire for a moment what is education. Webster defines it to be "a comprehension of all that series of instruction and discipline which is intended to enlighten the understanding, correct the temper, and form the manners and habits of youth, and fit them for usefulness in their future stations." He adds: "To give children a good education in manners, arts and sciences is important; to give them a religious education is indispensable."

But a more elaborate definition is given by one whom all will admit to have been among the ablest educators of his day, Horace Mann. Says he: "All intelligent thinkers upon the subject now utterly discard and repudiate the idea that reading and writing, with a knowledge of accounts, constitute education. The lowest claim which any intelligent man now prefers in its behalf, is that its domain extends over the three-fold nature of man; over his body, training it by the systematic and intelligent observance of those benign laws which secure health, impart strength, and prolong life; over his intellect, invigorating the mind, replenishing it with knowledge, and cultivating all those tastes which are allied to virtue; and over his moral and religious susceptibilities also, dethroning selfishness, enthroning conscience, leading the affections outwardly in good will toward man, and upward in gratitude and reverence to God."

This definition is complete and exhaustive. There can be no other correct view than that it extends to the entire three-fold nature of man. And education short of this must be only partial, limited, dwarfed, one-sided, and may be, in its operations and results, a greater curse than a blessing. Suppose, for example, we should disregard the mental and moral natures, and educate our youth only in the physical (and if we may neglect one, by the same rule we may another), what would be the result? There might be produced a race of athletes suited to the old games at Olympia, or a generation of Kings and Heenans, the champions of the modern prize ring—men largely animal, with feeble brains, and less morals. But again, should we develop the mind alone, disregarding the physical and the moral, we might have giant intellects, men who are able to wield the powers of government or shape the diplomacy of nations, yet they might be physical dwarfs, wrecks of disease, and, worse than all, moral pests upon the earth.

But still again, should we develop the physical and intellectual both, discarding the moral natures, as the enemies of our schools will allow, we might have stalwart bodies with giant minds, but no morals; mighty agents for evil, feeders on corruption, enemies to God, and destroyers of their race.

If State education must result in sending forth such characters as any or all these to the world, it will not take long to decide that it is a most dangerous and damaging institution, and ought at once to be abandoned. Were the question proposed to the people of the United States to-day—schools without morality and without Christianity, or no schools at all? the Christian people of the country ought not to ask a moment to decide, no schools at all. Better far that our noble fabric be demolished, than that it be converted into an enginery of immorality.

But let me here remind the advocates for an education divorced from all morals and religion, that their demands are not only absurd but an absolute impossibility. All nations on the face of the earth have some standard of morals. Some sort of morality is of necessity interwoven into their whole machinery of government, and to attempt to set up an institution of education without that morality would be like setting up a machine without its master-wheel, or an engine without its driver.

If it be a Mormon country, the government and all its institutions are founded on the basis, and administered according to the standard of a Mormon morality. Even its trade, its manufactories, its improvements, its trials before courts of justice, its pains and penalties, all, all are in accordance with Mormon right. If it teaches its children at all, it must teach them according to the standard of Mormon morals.

It is precisely so in Mohammedan countries, and in all Pagan countries, and can it be less so in a Christian land? Verily not. To attempt a system of education in any country, wholly divorced from the morality and religion of that country, is not only unphilosophical, but it is irrational. Were education only the combination of letters, and giving to these when combined a certain sound (little more than we could teach a parrot), or were it in addition the tracing of these letters upon paper; in other words, were it only the art of reading and writing, it might be separated from all morality and religion; but when we remember that these are not education at all, but only the mechanical apparatus by which the child is enabled to acquire it, we dare assert that the moment you enter the domain of education, that moment you unavoidably have to do with some standard of morals.

The meaning of many of the choicest words in our language is inseparably connected with morality and religion; for example, such words as just and true, and right and wrong, in a Christian land, differ infinitely from the same words in a Mormon, a Mohammedan, or Pagan country. And it is absolutely impossible to teach a child the meaning of them in a Christian land, without teaching it according to the Christian moral standard. If morals and religion are to be abolished from our schools, not a few of our choicest and best words must go out in the same abolition sentence.

But could a child be taught the meaning of words, there is not a step in science, there is not a step in philosophy, there is not a grade in history, that can be taken without a standard of morals. The effort to secularize our schools is only a covert attack upon their life principles, a deadly aim at their very existence. The heart purpose of the projectors is not written on the forefront of their movement. It is deeper than it proposes. As infidelity always does, it is fighting under a mask. David Hume left some infidel manuscripts with directions that they should be printed and published after his death. Says Dr. Johnson: "He loaded a blunderbuss, directed it against Christianity, and sneaked into the grave leaving another to fire it off." No less sneaking is the confederacy of the Jesuit and Jew, infidel and atheist, in their attacks upon the Bible in our schools. They are no friends of each other. They are really not in sypmathy. They have not the same ultimate object in view; but they have stricken hands like Herod and Pontius Pilate in the common work of crucifying Christ. The Jew would not object to the Bible if it were his own part of it. The Roman Catholic does not want a school system without religion. He has never said so; he dare not. To ask it would be to belie the tradition of his church for sixteen hundred years. Archbishop Purcell has given the animus of the movement on the part of the Catholics. Says he: "The entire government of public schools in which Catholic youth are educated cannot be given over to the civil power. We, as Catholics, cannot approve of that system of education for youth which is apart from instruction in the Catholic faith and the teaching of the Church." It is not *a* Bible the Catholic opposes so much in the schools as it is *the* Bible. It is not religion he opposes, but it is Protestanism; and so deep is his hatred to that, he will join with infidel and atheist in their opposition to all religion, in order to put it down.

It is safe to say that the Jesuit has a secret and concealed purpose to overthrow our entire school system, in the hope of securing pure and unmixed Catholic schools, untainted with the breath, or presence, or influence, of Protestantism. It is no slander to say that Roman Catholics have been the persistent and untiring enemies of our schools, and gladly embraced the opportunity to strike hands with any party or parties in their destruction.

But bound together, Jew and Jesuit, infidel and atheist, they have made the attack. By a counter-movement on the part of the friends of our school system, the matter has been carried into the arena of law. The question is stated, can we have the Bible in our schools by law? Is it in accordance with the genius of our Government? This question has already stood the test of debate before the Superior Court of Cincinnati, where some of the ablest lawyers of Ohio spent their strength for four days. The Constitution of Ohio was searched from preface to conclusion, in section, paragraph, and clause, to find some legal basis for the retention of the Bible. The search was not in vain. It provides as follows :

"Religion, morality, and knowledge being essentially necessary to good government and the happiness of mankind, schools, and the means of instruction, shall be forever encouraged by legislative provision, not inconsistent with the rights of conscience," etc.

On that constitutional provision was based the affirmative decision of the question. We hold the Bible in the schools of Ohio because of the word "religion" in our Constitution. But did the opponents submit to the decision ? By no means. They are determined to carry it to the last limit of law. They appealed it to the Supreme Court of Ohio, where it now awaits its trial and decision before the highest tribunal of that State. We believe when it is decided there it must be in our favor, because we have a constitutional guarantee for it. But when this question, agitated as it is now in many of the States, shall, as it must ultimately, come before the Supreme Court of the United States, where is the guarantee ? Where is the section, clause, or syllable, that gives any more right to read the Protestant Bible than the Koran or the writings of Confucius? There is not in all that, in many respects, noble instrument a word of preference for the Christian Bible ; not a line that authorizes its use, or will protect the reading of it in our schools.

With these facts before us—the defects of the Constitution on the one hand, and the enemy pressing furiously his attack upon the other—what is our line of duty? One of two things we must and will be compelled to do. Either give up the Bible to the enemy, yield it willingly, for logically we must, or else make our Constitution so that it will guarantee its use.

Christian men and women, which shall we do ? Yield our Bible ? Take it out of the hands of our children ? Turn our schools over into heathenism ? Blot the name of God out of our school-books ? Put away the name of Christ, and instead of Christian substitute Pagan morals ? Are you ready for that ? Men and women of Christian America, what say you ? I take the honest faces and the earnest hearts of this Convention in response. I take the four to five hundred delegates here, as the representatives of a vast multitude all over the land, gathering, growing, swelling, like the onward tide of the ocean, whose voices shall ere long be as the voice of many waters, when they shall come forward and utter their demand, "Amend, Amend the Constitution."

And now a word only to our opponents, to the "liberal" enemies of God and His Bible.

The Christian features of our schools, God helping us, we mean to maintain. We shall suffer the Bible to be torn from our children's hands and hearts only when we are overpowered and vanquished in the struggle.

Parker Pillsbury, while striving to excite opposition to our last Convention in Cincinnati, expressed his greatest alarm at the movement, because amongst its advocates were the descendants of those old religious heroes who, said he, "never beat upon the drum-head the hollow sound of retreat." We can assure Mr. Pillsbury and his confederates that into the vocabulary of this movement the word retreat has never come, and more than that it never shall. We cannot go back, and if we could God forbid we ever should. We believe it is the cause of God and cannot fail. It has the almightiness of Christianity in it, and shall ere long prove triumphant as certainly as that Christianity is true.

And in the firm, unwavering, undying faith in its ultimate triumph we mean with God's help to press on; not satisfied with its accomplishment in this country alone, we shall contribute our mite towards its realization in all lands, and shall tell our children to tell their children and their children's children never to give up the struggle until every knee shall bow, of things in heaven and things in earth, and things under the earth, and every tongue shall confess that Jesus Christ is Lord, to the Glory of God the Father.

Adjourned to meet at 7½ o'clock in the evening.

CLOSING SESSION.

The Convention re-assembled at 7½ o'clock, and was opened with prayer, the President in the chair.

The Committee on Permanent Organization was appointed a Committee to nominate officers for the National Association for the ensuing year.

Dr. Jonathan Edwards, of Peoria, Ill., was introduced and delivered the following address:

ADDRESS OF DR. EDWARDS.

Mr. President: I suppose we may as well begin at the beginning, even if some things be said which have been already said, and even if I repeat some things which were said at former conventions. Repetition is sometimes good. Even "pure minds" are the better for being "stirred up by way of remembrance."

We have formed an association to effect an amendment to the Constitution of the United States. Our proposed amendment does not touch to change—much less to abrogate—one of the truths, the principles or the features of that great instrument. Nor does it imply that we are wanting in appreciation of it; that we are dissatisfied or are restless under its working hitherto. Whoever likes the Constitution will find that we like it, and the institutions that have grown up under it, in the same measure and probably for the same good reasons. He will find us joined with him in the loyal support of all the good that is in it, its implied assertion of the rights of man and its wise provision for the growth of the nation. For such political wisdom given to our fathers we devoutly thank God; and it is our conviction and our boast that this Constitution is the best national charter recorded on the pages of history. But our fathers were not infallible, and the Constitution which they made for us was not perfect. Our nation's growth and experience have suggested several important amendments which have been already adopted; and, as it seems to us, the time has come to discuss the adoption of another. There are certain evils and certain signs of coming evil which give us anxiety. These evils and evil omens we trace back to an omission in the Constitution, and it is evident that if this omission be supplied the evils will be averted. And this is what we propose to do. Our amendment, like all the others, is suggested by our experience, and, however it may seem to be late in the day, can never be out of date. There is no mention of God in the Constitution, no word which recognizes His sovereignty over human affairs or His interest in them. One of the great—one of the chief characteristics of our people at the time they entered into national compact is thus ignored. The underlying faith of our forefathers, a faith which must have given life and shape to their politics and their institutions, is thus not alluded to. I repeat, this is the omission which now engages our attention and which we wish to supply. We feel that such an omission does injustice to the people, who, because of it, are but partially described and but partially represented in their Constitution. It would seem as if they had not understood how great and how grave was the work of nation-making in which they were engaged, and that they gave to it only such earnestness as showed their desire for safety, peace and wealth—mere material interests—though our forefathers, as we know, were a serious, thoughtful people, accustomed to do everything of a public nature in the name and the fear of God; and though they settled the land and made their laws from the beginning as much for religious faith as for civil freedom, or rather, for the freedom of religious faith.

It has been thought that this omission was mere oversight. Indeed, tradition says that Alexander Hamilton told a minister of the Gospel in this city, on his return from the Convention, that the mention of God had been entirely forgotten! I wonder that great man did not call to mind the Bible warning to "all the nations that forget God." But whether they forgot it, or whether there was a secret intent to imitate France, the nation which at that day was the ideal of political progress as well as of politeness and science, it is not necessary, not important now to settle. It is more important to correct it than to account for it. The fact is that the Constitution is silent on the subject of God and religion, and we urge that this is a wrong, an injustice, a vicious impolicy.

The newspapers say we are trying to put God into the Constitution. Well, that does describe in part our aim and our work. It is bad for anything to be without God. Everything is the better for having Him in it. As the venerable father who addressed you last evening said, in words so fervid and so eloquent, I am in favor of putting or finding God everywhere; in the country and in the town, in the parlor and in the workshop, every day as well as Sunday. But there is also another thing we want to put into the Constitution. We want to put the people into it, the people in full, the people with their deep and noble reverence for God as the Greatest and the Best, and for His word as the underlying and paramount law. In these traits they certainly are not there now. If the Convention had only prefaced the Constitution with "In the name of God, Amen," as the Puritans did in the colony compact they drew up and signed in the cabin of the Mayflower, possibly this movement of ours had never been made.

Our proposed Amendment is confined chiefly and almost exclusively to the Preamble of the Constitution. We wish it there distinctly declared that this people found this Government with a reverent regard to God and His revealed will.

Strictly speaking, the Preamble is not the Constitution. It is a solemn statement that goes before the Constitution, in which the people who make the Constitution describe themselves, define their aims and their work, and so, as it were, announce and introduce themselves to the nations of the earth. It is mere statement, I admit, but it is a statement of facts which are important, and which are of practical value ; such facts as furnish a good point of departure for those who shall afterwards make or expound laws. For instance, the Preamble, as it now stands, indicates that the nation is, as yet, but imperfectly compacted ; that, after ten years of such life and progress as could be secured under the confederation, it is found necessary "to form a more perfect union"—intimating that all after legislation to weaken or dissolve this union will be unconstitutional. This union, with sundry great moral, social and civil benefits depending upon it, "the people," (not the States,) the Preamble tells us, met in convention to secure, and to this end ordained the Constitution, and we have found in our national history presumptions emanating originally from this Preamble, working mightily and continually in favor of the rights of the people, and in favor of national unity, integrity and eminent domain, as against State sovereignty, sectional interests, excessive official power and patronage, and the influence of overgrown corporations. Just here we propose to do our work ; that, among these preliminary statements of the source from which the Constitution emanates, there be one which refers to the religious convictions under which our people acted in convention. What we shall gain by such a statement will be a general presumption in favor of Christian morals and usages.

Thus far we have not touched the body of the Constitution. We have but modified the portico, yet already the building is more proportionate and more enduring for what we have done. There will follow, for mere consistency's sake, one or two slight changes in the Constitution, yet these are only remote and incidental, not at all essential, and not interfering with the rights of conscience any more than it now does.

The first and principal change that occurs to me as proper to be made is in the prescribed form of oath. The President must be sworn into office—that is, he must say, "I do solemnly swear." This is now his oath. Kissing a book is a custom, not a law, I believe ; but, whether this ceremony be custom or law, it is unmeaning, undignified, childish and ridiculous. But merely saying "I swear" is not swearing. It may indicate the thing he would do if he could, but it is not the thing itself. If I say I steal, does that convict me of theft ? Does not the law require proof of some overt act? So of swearing. There must be an act and a formula to constitute an oath, and for these we look into our Bible. The right hand is to furnish the act: as it is said of base, unworthy men, "Their right hand is a right hand of falsehood." And the name of God is to furnish the formula: "Thou shalt fear the Lord thy God . . and shalt swear by His name." This is not a mere question of unimportant forms, or of trifling details. It is a great peace measure, since "an oath for confirmation is an end of all strife." It is a measure of high prudence, a guarantee for fidelity in administration, in contracts and in witness bearing. And it ought to be so constructed as to form a sacred bond between the conscience of him who takes it and the Throne of God, the bar of final accountability. If the oath be not the foundation of society, it is at least the cement with which those foundations are laid.

I do not now think of any other change that would be necessary under our Amendment in the body of the Constitution.

But the Constitution being now silent upon the subject of religion, as has been said, it is urged against us that our movement is unnecessary. The people are believers in God and Christianity, and the statesmen, at least the politicians, will always be only too careful to legislate in accordance with their faith as well as with their tastes and their interests. So, as you have already heard it well stated, the people were believers in liberty, but for want of some constitutional utterance that was definite and decisive we had to pass through a civil war of frightful porportions ere it was settled that freedom was national among us. Shall we wait to learn in some similar schooling that Christianity is one of our formal characteristics?

But, in fact, the Constitution is not silent upon the subject of religion. I have said that its silence was an injustice and an evil, but the great grievance is that it has spoken and spoken wrong. What you have given you in your law books as the Constitution is silent, but this is not the whole of that document. There are other chapters of the Constitution which are not generally seen by the people, perhaps not even suspected. Treaties made with foreign nations are counted as parts of the Constitution and possess the same power as the rest of the Constitution to render null and void anything contrary to them in the laws or the constitutions of the States severally. Now, it was stated last evening, that early in the history of our Government our diplomats abroad misrepresented us to a foreign court by saying we were a nation without any religion at all. But the case is far worse than this. In one or two treaties, which our President and Senate made for us in due form, we have given to the world as fundamental law with us that the United States is in no sense founded upon the Christian religion, and, in effect, that our institutions will not prove embarrassing to a good Mussulman. We stand upon our constitutional record as not materially different from a nation of Mohammedans. And is this no injustice, no libel? It is both; and our movement for the Religious Amendment indicates that we are not disposed to submit to it.

It is said, if you make these alterations they will necessarily be followed by a great deal of legislation. Well, if so, let us have it. The people who vote for the amendment will also vote the laws which may be needed to give it efficacy. No trouble, no disturbance of the peace need be apprehended. But what legislative difficulties are anticipated? First, the union of Church and State. Truly this is a giant evil. It is well worth while to give warning of anything and everything that threatens, however remotely, to bring that about, and we will all join you in doing so. I suppose there could not be found a corporal's guard in this large convention that look upon such complications and corruptions as a union of Church and State would amount to with any other feeling than detestation and dread. We all sincerely and most heartily repudiate any design or desire to effect it. As promptly as any one, we would both resent and resist it. And yet it might not be amiss to suggest that injurious relations with the Church are not the only entanglements the State has to fear and the patient has to guard against. China is a vast speeimen of a purely paternal government. Old Rome identified state and army, citizen and soldier. Carthage was all for commerce. The French say that modern England is a nation of shop-keepers, and the Company of India combines administration and traffic. Do you dislike and dread state and family, state and army, state and shop, as well as state and church? All these in their turn are dangers to which we are exposed, yet who sounds the alarm, who prepares the protest, who rallies the opposition? It is just possible that the outcry against Church and State may spring rather from hatred to revealed religion than from an intelligent patriotism. But where is the sign, the omen of such Church and State mischief coming upon us? Who will begin and who will finish this union of Church and State? If you think the Roman Catholic can do it in spite of the watchfulness of the Protestant; or that one Protestant sect can do it amid the jealousy of all the other sects; or that all these sects would combine to effect a joint union with the state, you have a notion of human nature and of church nature different from what I have. Church and State in union, then, are forever impossible here, and, were it never so easy, we all repudiate it on principle. There are enduring, ever valid reasons against it. But religion and state is another thing. That is possible. That is a good thing—and that is what we aim to make a feature in our institutions.

The languages of the earth are taught in a variety of grammars. It may be useless, if not impracticable for the State to link itself with a grammar, but it will be worse than useless, it will be wholly impossible to do without a language. There are many languages spokeu in our great country, yet here the State elects English to be its official tongue. It has never passed a law to this effect, but the language of the first settlers has been quietly accepted and used until at length it has the general force of law. The foreigner may speak what tongue he pleases, but he must act the citizen in English, he must vote in English, he must have laws drafted, debated and enacted in English.

There are many schools of medicine—homeopathic, allopathic, hydropathic, and what not. It might be exceedingly injudicious for the State to commit itself to either of these and to establish it exclusively; but medicine, the healing art, it must recognize, and from time to time employ for its servants and its soldiers. There must to this extent be State and Medicine.

In like manner we want State and Religion—and we are going to have it. It shall be that so far as the affairs of State require Religion, it shall be revealed Religion, the Religion of Jesus Christ. The Christian oath and Christian morality shall have in this land "an undeniable legal basis."

We use the word Religion in its proper sense, as meaning a man's personal relation of faith and obedience to God. There is another use of the word, a narrow ecclesiastical use of it, brought down to us from the Middle Ages and from Popery. They said a man was religious who entered into renewed and redoubled relations to the Church, as when he became a monk, for instance. It is possible this was the sense contemplated by our Constitution when it prohibited religious tests as a qualification for holding office. The State determined to take no part and to show no preference among the controversies of the Church, nor to make the Church in any of its usages or requirements a condition for her honors and her services. But, as we use it, Religion is not the Church, but a deep principle, like life, which underlies and pervades the State and the family as well as the Church. We hold that there may be religious families and religious states as well as religious churches, and that families and states, as well as churches, are all the better for being religious.

Now, we are warned that to engraft this doctrine upon the Constitution will be found oppressive; that it will infringe the rights of conscience; and we are told that there are Atheists, Deists, Jews and Seventh-day Baptists who would be sufferers under it. I accept it as a compliment that we are called upon to consider objections of this sort, if there be any ground for them. We are the conscience party, the free conscience party. We are the very people to be held responsible if we trespass upon the conscience of others. And it will be found that we do not intend to do this, and that we do not do it in fact.

The parties whose conscience we are charged with troubling, taken altogether, are but few in number. This determines nothing as to who is right, but the fact remains, and is worthy of note, that, taken altogether, they amount to but a small fraction of our citizenship. They are not even as many as those among us who do not speak the English language.

And then, further, they are almost wholly of foreign importation, and that of comparatively recent date, so that they did not share in the first settlement of this country; they did not brave the hardships, they did not profess the principles which have made that settlement memorable. They never, anywhere, developed, or even dreamed of such a nationality as ours, such a written guarantee for stability, liberty and progress. In the lands where they lived before coming hither, they had less of liberty than they enjoy here, but their notions of conscience and liberty were too vague for them even to feel themselves aggrieved. They breathed no protests, they suffered no martyrdom. These come to us, who have made for them the freest land ever beneath the sun, and warn us not to infringe their rights of conscience—rights which they had to come here even to learn! They are afraid that those who taught them freedom are going to oppress them!

Well, let us attend to the case. They do not, as yet, feel oppressed. They will not pretend that, on the whole, they are not very well off—better off than before they came—as well off as they expected to be. Under our present Constitution and laws they can vote, can hold property, can marry, can plead and be impleaded, can fare better than in any other country. But they cannot do everything, have everything, be everything. Well, in this they are not alone. There are many rights and privileges which are but imperfectly accorded to all our citizens. There are many things which we may not do, however conscience clear we may be of our right, our interest, or our pleasure in them. We may not smoke a cigar in the streets of Boston.* We may not buy a lot among the fine houses of Broadway, or the fashionable avenues of New York, and there set up and operate a foundery, a tin-shop, a bone-boiling establishment or a soap chandlery. If we try it we shall find both ourselves and our business treated as a nuisance. People do not like the smoke, the noise, the fumes of such establishments. The majority are against you, and in this country and all republics majorities govern. To be in a minority involves more or less of inconvenience. In business, in politics, in fashion, in morals and in religion, whoever differs materially from the majority will certainly be made to feel it more or less in due time. All law, all government, will press somewhere occasionally, and it is the good citizen who maintains both his conscience and his independence by submitting to the pressure. Our objectors, as I said, are not alone in their disabilities.

One class of our earliest and best citizens is composed of Quakers, who are in name and in principle opposed to all war. It is doubtful whether a Quaker can, with a good conscience, be President of the United States and thus be Commander-in-Chief of the Army and Navy. Yet the majority of our people thus far remain firm in the purpose to keep an army and navy, and, what is more,

* Such was the law not long since enforced in Boston.

on occasion to use them. There is also another body of our citizens of good stock and well ordered lives and sound principles, men who in other lands were identified with freedom of conscience—we heard from them this morning, the Covenanters—who in this land do not feel themselves at liberty even to vote. And some of our countrymen are conscientious monarchists. The State protects all who are peaceable, but it cannot do otherwise than reflect the mind of the majority. Our objectors, then, may learn that they are merely a body of men who are in their turn feeling the inconvenience of dissent. And they may be reminded that under our proposed Amendment all the essentials of their citizenship will be none the less secure to them than they are now.

The Atheist is a man who denies the being of a God and a future life. To him mind and matter are the same, and time is the be-all and the end-all of consciousness and of character.

The Deist admits God, but denies that He has any such personal control over human affairs as we call providence, or that He ever manifests Himself and His will in a Revelation.

The Jew admits God, Providence, and Revelation, but rejects the entire scheme of Gospel redemption by Jesus Christ as sheer imagination, or—worse —sheer imposture.

The Seventh-day Baptists believe in God and Christianity, and are conjoined with the other members of this class by the accident of differing with the mass of Christians upon the question of what precise day of the week shall be observed as holy.

These all are, for the occasion, and so far as our Amendment is concerned, one class. They use the same arguments and the same tactics against us. They must be counted together, which we very much regret, but which we cannot help. The first named is the leader in the discontent and in the outcry—the atheist, to whom nothing is higher or more sacred than man, and nothing survives the tomb. It is his class. Its labors are almost wholly in his interest; its success would be almost wholly his triumph. The rest are adjuncts to him in this contest. They must be named from him; they must be treated as, for this question, one party. Now look at it—look at this controversy. The question is not between opinions that differ, but opinions that are opposite, that are contradictory, that mutually exclude each other. It is between Christianity and Infidelity. It is between Theism and Atheism, between the acknowledgment of a God and the denial that there is any God. We cannot too seriously ponder this, since the rights of conscience are held to be involved. The atheist does not believe in the soul; he denies that there is any such thing as conscience; yet he comes to those who confess both to insist upon his rights of conscience! I have a few plain, earnest words about all this.

I do not believe that every man is an atheist who says he is one. I distinguish between minds that doubt or deny the existence of God, and those who doubt or deny the sufficiency of the logic usually employed to prove it. And I love to think genuine atheism impossible to the human soul. But now bring forward your atheist, your man who confesses to neither God, angel, nor spirit, your man who believes in all unbelief, and in nothing else, and I know at once what his position is. His religion is irreligion; his morals are only natural morals—the morals of the body, the animal in man, which, in his view, is all there is of man. His speculations do not rove or float among the dreams of philosophy, but they run into the concrete forms of politics—into the platforms of parties and the enactments of legislatures. Atheism is always political. What are the rights of the atheist? I would tolerate him as I would tolerate a poor lunatic, for in my view his mind is scarcely sound. So long as he does not rave, so long as he is not dangerous, I would tolerate him. I would tolerate him as I would a conspirator. The atheist is a dangerous man. He not only rejects and opposes my faith, but he aims to overturn every institution, and to dissolve every relationship growing out of my faith. He would destroy the very foundations, pull down everything, and build up nothing. But he shall be tolerated. He may live and go free, hold his lands and enjoy his home, he may even vote, but for any higher, more advanced citizenship, he is, as I hold, utterly disqualified. And we are aiming, not to increase, but to render definite his disqualification; to give to our Government and all our free institutions a guarantee that he shall never have control over them. Yes, to this extent I will tolerate the atheist, but no more. Why should I? The atheist does not tolerate me. He does not smile either in pity or in scorn upon my faith. He hates my faith, and he hates me for my faith. He is bent on exterminating me and my faith altogether. "Crush the wretch!" said Voltaire of my Saviour and His cause. And this is still the atheist's motto and his aim. I have received letters and tracts which show this very clearly. Were I to read to you the shocking blasphemies, the words of hate and of murder which they contain, you would shudder in horror. He means to make all these words good among us as soon as he can. And I am asked to accord rights of conscience to a man who says to me, "Come, let me show you how I can use the knife with which I purpose one day to cut your throat." "Come, let me explain to you the force of some nitro-glycerine which I have prepared to blow you up!" I can be as calm and as willing in the one case as in the other. And I am asked to tolerate the atheist's creed under peril of violating the rights of conscience. And this tolerating of atheism means, I suppose, that our Constitution and laws shall be so framed as to imply that there is as much of truth, probability and good in atheism as in Christianity! Tolerate atheism in this sense, sir? Never, never! We know what atheism is, and what atheism does. We know what it builds, and how it operates with its "Natural Morals," its "Death an Eternal Sleep," its "Liberty, Equality, Fraternity." Twice, at least, in the world's history has it shown what it is capable of doing. Twice across the plains of gay and sunny France has it driven its car of progress, and the whole track has been rapine, and blasphemy, and blood. I can tolerate difference and discussion; I can tolerate heresy and false religion; I can debate the use of the Bible in our common schools; the taxation of church property, the propriety of chaplaincies and the like, but there are some questions past debate. Tolerate atheism, sir? There is nothing out of hell that I would not tolerate as soon. The atheist may live, as I said, but, God helping us, the taint of his destructive creed shall not defile any of the civil institutions of all this fair land! Let us repeat, atheism and Christianity are contradictory terms. They are incompatible systems. They cannot dwell together on the same continent. And let us note that this atheism among us is busy. It is aggressive, with societies, with organs, with agents; with their papers and their preachers. But recently they have imported a man, the papers say, at a salary of $15,000, to go through the land lecturing and organizing, telling us how to Germanize and un-Americanize our country. Their organizations raise money, issue publications, form public sentiment and secure votes against our Sunday laws, our blasphemy laws, our temperance laws, our cruelty laws, our laws for social purity and home sanctity, our oath-sealed guaranty for truth and fidelity, and to bring us all down to mere natural morals. We too must organize and make effort. "The Lord of Hosts is with us, the God of Jacob is our refuge!"

Another anticipated difficulty which is urged against us is to determine what Bible to recognize. This difficulty is but imaginary. There is but one Bible. What is called the Catholic or the Protestant Bible is but the Catholic or the Protestant version of the one original Bible. And with every strong conviction that the Protestant version is the better one, I am free to say that any Bible is better than no Bible.

And yet another objection is that the laws of Moses will have to be re-enacted and enforced among us, and that these laws are not at all fitted to our times, our freedom, our civilization. I confess that I am not at all afraid of Moses. I find among his institutions the germs of our own glorious Republic, and the provisions and the spirit of our best laws. But the objectors do not seem to have read the Bible enough to see what a self-interpreting book it is. It records a prophecy and afterwards records its fulfilment. It records a promise and afterwards states when and how the bestowment was effected. It records a ritual and afterwards records what abrogated it and took its place. It gives of itself the clue to distinguish what is of enduring value and moral obligation from what is local, typical, transitory. Now, if there be anything in the laws of Moses which the coming of Christ and the subsequent overthrow of Judaism did not abrogate, let them be pointed out—there cannot be many of them—and we are prepared to accept them and have them re-enacted.

Thus much as to objections and objectors.

As to our movement and our National Association, I have to say:

1. That it is most catholic. It is a matter of general interest. It equally concerns Democrat and Republican, Catholic and Protestant, Unitarian and Trinitarian. I do not say that all these are actually, as yet, combined in it; but all might be thus combined without any compromise of what is distinctive among them, and I trust that ere long they will be. No broader platform was ever erected in American politics.

2. It is a practical measure. It is no dream of mere enthusiasts or fanatics. It does not aim simply to nationalize some shibboleth of some sect. It presents not a question of words, but of underlying comprehensive principles. If these can in due form be secured, it seems to us that the foundations of our nation's character will be secured, the law of our nation's beneficent and unending progress will be secured.

3. It is an essential measure. It is as essential as the Oath is essential, as Christian morals are essential, as Christianity is essential. It will not do to say, we had better leave things as they now are. Things are in a state of change, of transition; they will not stay as they now are. It will not do to say, let us trust the voice of a Christian people for the perpetuity of Christian principles and usages among us; for, in despite of their voice and their influence, the moulding, over-riding force of our national Constitution has more and more eliminated the notion of God and of moral character from our recent State Constitutions and from the decisions of our courts. If we do not carry

this measure, we take the side of atheism. You are called upon, fellow-citizens, to make your election between Christianity and Atheism. "Under which king, Bezonian?" You cannot be too soon in making your response. I cannot doubt what your decision will be.

Our movement means business. We are, as yet, possibly not perfect in all the details of our great measure. We are willing to receive suggestions from our friends. We are willing to gather hints even from our enemies. But we mean to carry this measure if it takes all that ten generations you heard mentioned last evening. Our faith is in God, in His word and in the co-operation of all good men.

I believe I have thus touched upon as many points as I dare without the fear of trespassing upon your long patience.

The following address was next delivered by Professor J. R. W. Sloane, D. D., of Alleghany, Pa.

ADDRESS OF PROFESSOR J. R. W. SLOANE.

The object which has assembled this Convention is one whose importance it would be very difficult to exaggerate. The open, distinct and avowed purpose of the "National Reform Association" is to secure such an amendment to the Constitution of the United States as shall furnish a legal basis for legislation upon those elements of our national life that are specifically Christian; such, for example, as Christian marriage; the Sabbath as a day of rest for the laboring man, and of peaceful worship for the religious man; the Bible in the schools; the judicial oath in our courts of justice; chaplains in our army, navy, and public institutions under the control of Government; special days of fasting and thanksgiving, etc.

That a free people should be somewhat sensitive respecting changes in their Constitution is at once natural and proper. The Constitution represents stable government, and stable government is essential to national prosperity and progress. It is not desirable that frequent changes should be made in the National Charter. Nevertheless, the Constitution of a free Government not only may, but must, from time to time, be altered and amended according to the varying and progressive changes of the national life; otherwise it will prove a barrier to national progress, and eventually provoke resistance and revolution. Plant an oak in a vase, and either the vase will kill the oak, or the oak will burst the vase. The garments of the boy of fifteen will not do for the muscular, developed man of twenty-five. The Constitution framed for the thirteen colonies before the steamship, the locomotive, or the telegraph had appeared, will not meet the requirements of our nation to-day, into which so many new forces, both moral and physical, have entered. The only appropriate question which can be asked is, as to the importance, necessity and practicability of the proposed amendment. If it meet some great felt and conscious necessity of the nation, if it be clearly foreseen that its adoption will be productive of beneficent results, then it is at once the dictate, both of reason and of statesmanship, that it be accepted. That such an emergency has arisen is the profound conviction of many of the most thoughtful minds of the country. Our fathers designed to found here a great, free and Christian republic. We have made it free from ocean to ocean, from the Lakes to the Gulf; and we are now resolved, with the divine assistance, to secure its Christian features against all the disorganizing forces which assail them, and give them the guarantee of a specific declaration in the National Constitution. There is no one element of the national life distinctively Christian which is not assailed, nor one which is not called in question, and the right and reason of its existence under the Constitution denied. These assaults, taken in connection with the alarming corruption in political life, have created a deep and wide-spread concern for the stability of our Government. The right to read the Bible in the public schools is appealed to the higher courts in the State of Ohio. The same right is denied to the schools of New York by the decision of the State Superintendent. Sabbath laws are either abrogated or rapidly becoming a dead letter on the statute book. The abrogation of the judicial oath in our courts of justice is loudly urged, and all this pressed on the ground of constitutional right. The conflict is upon us; the issue is made. The necessity for making constitutional provision against infidel demands is as urgent as it was a few years ago for making such provision against slavery. The view which we urge upon this subject is no new thing. Five years after the adoption of the present Constitution, Rev. Dr. John Mason, of this city—perhaps the greatest pulpit orator of America, the intimate friend and eulogist of Alexander Hamilton, according to the statement of his son to the present speaker, the most prominent of the framers of the Constitution—used these words: "Should the citizens of America be as irreligious as her Constitution, we have reason to fear lest the Governor of the Universe, who will not be treated with indignity by a people any more than by individuals, overturn from the foundation the fabric we have been rearing, and crush us to atoms in the wreck."

It is proper, also, to remark that this movement rests upon the profoundest principles of political philosophy, as well as upon the pure precepts of Christian morality, and is, therefore, thoroughly logical and consistent with itself.

That government is a divine, and not a human institution, is affirmed by all political writers whose opinion is of any value upon the subject. To name them is to name all those who have obtained eminence in political science in our own country: Lieber, late of Columbia College; Tayler Lewis, of Union; Prof. Seelye, of Amherst, the scholar and thinker of New England; Mulford, the author of that able political work, "The Nation;" O. A. Brownson, author of "The American Republic," not to mention others of equal ability on these subjects, some of whom are with us in this Convention.

Governments are not made; they grow. They are not of man, nor of the will of man, but of God. They arise under the operation of God's providential laws, and are created as moral persons for the accomplishment of moral ends. "The nation is not a confused collection of separate atoms, as grains of sand in a heap, and its increase is not through their accumulation. It has the unity of an organism, not the aggregation of a mass."

If Government be not divine, then it is merely a voluntary association, and may be dissolved like other voluntary associations, at the will of those who are thus united; but this theory would subvert society and lead to anarchy.

The experiment of the erratic Thoreau, had it been successful, would have proved him stronger than Massachusetts, stronger than the United States; would have proved the same as to every other individual under the Government, and, of course, would have subverted its very foundation.

We are born under government—live, act our little part, and die under it. We have no choice in the matter. We can no more escape from it than from the blue heavens above us. With reverence it may be said of government, as of its Author: "If I take the wings of the morning and dwell in the uttermost parts of the sea, even there shall Thy hand lead me, and Thy right hand hold me." There is no divine right of kings. There are no providential rulers supernaturally raised up to govern. There is, however, a divine right of government; it is of God through the people. Hence, rulers are accountable both to God and the people. When properly understood, "*vox populi, vox Dei*," is the embodiment of a political truth. This view of government is the only one that has the slightest claim to be considered philosophical and scientific, and makes our demand for a recognition of God in the Constitution not merely reasonable, but logical and necessary. The sciolists who have been in such eager haste to throw themselves in the path of this movement, have never made even an attempt at argument on fundamental principles. They are wise. Every other view of government is unscientific, disorganizing, anarchical and despotic. We embrace the opportunity to say to these gentlemen that platitudes about Puritanism, Jewish Theocracy, union of Church and State, religious persecution, &c., are arrows that fall harmless at our feet. A cause like this, resting on fundamental principles, is not to be arrested by such feeble weapons. We take their sneers and bind them as a wreath of honor around our brows. As to their opinions which they utter so oracularly, I would that they understood how little we regard them.

Not a few journals which betray their utter ignorance of the principles of political philosophy, treat the arguments for this movement with combined flippancy and arrogance. And the "New York *Independent!*" I have seen somewhere a story of a poor animal, on which a cruel devotee of science had been experimenting, that continued to wriggle for some three days after the brains were taken out of it. The brains were taken out of the *Independent* some two or three years ago, but it wriggles yet.

Again, governments are the subjects of God's immutable laws, whether they ackowledge the fact or not. Their unbelief cannot make void the purpose of God. The government is not the people, nor the people the government, although the one is not without the other. There is one law for the individual, and another for the government—a judgment of the individual and a judgment of the nation. As moral persons, they are the subjects of God's moral laws. There is no future state of rewards and punishment for nations; hence they receive their doom or their chastisement in this world. Rome advanced her conquests until she embraced the civilized world. Her victorious eagles hovered over the finest portions of three-quarters of the globe. She fell, not because of any dark or fatal necessity compelling the rise and fall of empires, but because of her own crimes. The huge and bloated carcass was rotten at the heart; barbarous invasion but completed what internal corruption had begun. The Goth, the Vandal and the Hun thundered at her gates. Her pomp, her glory and her multitudes went down to the dust. God's laws were violated, and God's ministers of vengeance executed upon her the penalty. We need not go to the nations of antiquity for our examples.

But a few years have passed since we were, as a nation, the subject of one of the most severe national chastisements that has befallen any nation of modern times. We were in the full tide of national prosperity, as men judge national prosperity; but there was a gross national sin resting upon us. Suddenly the clouds of confusion gathered over us; the Lord God thundered in the heavens, and there the Highest gave his voice, hailstones and coals of fire; He sent out his lightnings, and smote us; He lifted up the waves of His wrath, and rolled them upon us. The land trembled beneath the shock of contending armies, and the earth drank in the blood of the slain. When "those war-clouds rolling dun" had passed away, three billions of treasure had perished; a million lives had been sacrificed; there was not a house in which there was not one dead; the land was filled with a very great mourning, as the mourning of Hadad Rimmon in the Valley of Megiddon—Rachel weeping for her children, and refusing to be comforted. Can history furnish a more striking illustration of the punishment of a nation, coming directly from the hand of God for the violation of His law? There is nothing in this supernatural—nothing miraculous. It all occurs in accordance with the operation of laws which God has established. "*Facilis descensus Averni*," is true of a nation. "Ephraim is joined to his idols, let him alone."

Again, in the conduct of its policy, whether that policy relate to its own citizens, or to its relation to other nations, a nation is as much under obligation to obey the law of God as the humblest of its citizens. We have had a policy toward the Indian in the past. That policy we all admit to have been in many respects unjust. We have another policy at present—a policy of which our esteemed Chairman is an honored agent. This policy is distinctively *Christian*. The present results are several expensive Indian wars avoided, with their attendant waste of blood and treasure. We have had a policy toward the negro; a policy toward nations with whom we have been brought into various relations; a policy toward the Mormons; a policy toward the Chinaman, &c. What is the standard of national conduct in all these instances? Is our own will the rule, or is there a higher law by which we should be governed, and by which we will be tried? To ask these questions is to answer them. No thoroughly informed person will deny that a nation is a *moral* person. Great Britain and the United States meet in arbitration; the question between them is one of rights; an appeal to a standard must be made; that standard is the "Law of Nations," but of this law it may indeed be said that "it hath its seat in the bosom of God, and its voice is the harmony of the world." The "Law of Nations" is an expression of the divine justice, and rests ultimately upon the revealed will of God. The recognition on the part of a nation of its subordination to the law of God is the recognition simply of a demonstrated, accepted political truth.

There is no point upon which even intelligent persons appear to be more confused than upon the true end of government. The prevalent opinion is that government is simply a device for the preservation and furtherance of material interests. Jefferson's view was that its end was to prevent pockets being picked and legs from being broken; or, as it is more philosophically expressed, for the protection of life and property. We heard that eminent philanthropist, Gerritt Smith, when running as independent candidate for the governorship of the State of New York, say in this hall that government was simply the *watch-dog* lying at the door of the citizen to protect his property. An astute lawyer rose in the audience, and asked him what then was his opinion of the Public School system of the State, and he was compelled to answer that he did not believe education properly a function of government!

A moment's reflection is sufficient to convince any one both of the fallacy and inadequacy of such views. Formed in the moral sphere of the divine government, civil government must deal with the higher principles of human nature and with the higher interests of society. The family is formed according to its conception of the true character of that relation. The relation of parent and child is controlled and regulated by its laws. Every right, whether of property or of conscience, is secured or destroyed by its arrangement. Is there any interest of man which it does not affect? Any department of human action with which it does not directly or indirectly interfere? Whoever reflects upon it aright will be ready to say with Arnold of Rugby, that it is monstrous that such a power should recognize no authority higher than itself. This is a sufficient answer to the question so often asked, why a government should acknowledge God rather than a bank, railroad, or other corporation. Government is supreme. "*Diis immortalibus proximi sunt magistratus.*" There is no other power to interfere between it and the people. It would be eminently fitting that corporations of every kind should acknowledge God. The current maxim that governments have no souls indicates the corrupt sentiment that originates fraudulent "rings" and "corners." These corporations, however, are, as Blackstone says, merely "artificial persons;" they are limited to merely pecuniary interests, are subject to the sovereign power, and can be made or dissolved according to its pleasure. The government, however, is a different agent altogether; it knows no power higher than itself; it controls all, and is controlled by none. "Whom it will it kills, and whom it will it keeps alive." No power can interfere between it and the subject; its sentence is final and, save by itself, irreversible. For this reason, government by a majority recognizing no allegiance to God is a despotism as dangerous and as absolute as that of the purest autocracy the world has ever seen. On my way to this Convention I asked an eminent lawyer, a member of the Pennsylvania Constitutional Convention, "Why do you punish bigamy in Pennsylvania?" "Because it is a crime—a *malum in se.*" "According to what law?" "Of course," he replied, "the law of God as revealed in Christianity." This is the precise truth. Why not, then, acknowledge the law by which our legislation is and must be governed? A friend to whom I put the same question replied, that it should be punished for the good of society. But who is to judge? In Mohammedan countries polygamy prevails, not in their estimation a *malum*, but a *bonum in se*—a useful institution necessary to the good, perhaps the very existence, of society! Is it not plain that our legislation proceeds on principles purely *Christian* that to deny this fact, or to act on the denial, would subvert modern society? Thus it is manifest that this movement is not only *theoretical*, resting upon fundamental principles, but eminently *practical.* The law of marriage makes all the difference between Western and Oriental civilization. Polygamy, as an institution, rests in Mohammedan countries upon the Koran; but in Christian countries, upon the rule of Christ, "They twain shall be one flesh." If our Government is to know no distinction of religion, why shall we discriminate against the Mormon or Mohammedan on a principle which his religion does not forbid, nay, into which it enters as an essential element? To deny that we have a right to legislate on Christian principles is to deny a principle upon which our legislatures and courts are acting every day. The theory which we oppose, if logically carried out, would reduce men to a herd, and society to the wildest anarchy.

We are justly proud of our liberties; but whence have they come? From an ancestry thoroughly imbued with Christianity, men who shed their blood like water to secure the right to read the Word of God, and to worship Him according to its requirements. "O Liberty, what crimes have been committed in thy name!" said Madame Roland, as from the scaffold she raised her hands to Heaven. Let us remember that these crimes have been committed in the name of infidel liberty—not of a liberty regulated by the law of Christ. The open Bible, Pere Hyacinthe affirms to be the secret of the power and glory of America and Britain. Every step of progress which a nation makes is by taking up some Christian principle into the national life. French communism is the ideal of those who stand in the front ranks of our opponents—a horror which so alarms the French people of to-day that they willingly submit to almost any government which gives them security against its atrocities. The more a nation has of Christianity the freer it becomes, is a fact which admits of no exception since the days of Christ; and yet one would think, to hear certain newspapers talk, that it was of all other things to be dreaded and shunned. A decade will not in all probability pass until it will be seen that this contest is a struggle for civil and religious liberty against atheism and infidelity, those dire foes not only of God, but of man. I do not wish to exaggerate the evils of the hour. A great calamity has fallen upon us. We hang our heads with shame. Is there no remedy? Is there no balm in Gilead? Is there no physician there? Are not the leaves of the tree of life for the healing of this nation? I am aware that men say, "Look at your Christian Statesmen!" That some of those implicated in these recent disgraceful transactions have made some sort of Christian profession is currently reported; that they were among the most trusted of our public men all admit. When I was in Chicago, after the great conflagration, I saw how the apparently strongest and most durable structures had melted like wax in that awful furnace;—those that remained standing, crumbled and defaced as though smitten by all the storms of ruin for a thousand years. What must have been the intensity of that conflagration in which they perished? When we see men go down like those whose names for very pity we cannot mention, we may infer how great the temptation to which they have been exposed, and find an additional argument for the necessity of applying a radical remedy to the existing state of politics in our country. There is no charm in words, but there is omnipotence in principles. Our amendment would elevate government into the sphere of a high moral duty, and remove it from the domain now occupied by the stock exchange and the speculators' "corner." Its tendency must be to raise up a class of public men influenced by moral considerations, and accepting office as a duty to be discharged, rather than as a door of admission to an opportunity for the accumulation of boundless personal wealth.

What other remedy is proposed that has not again and again been tried and failed? Is it not time to make one earnest and united effort to infuse a new power into government, that may transform politics from a reckless game into a sacred trust?

There are other questions of a more immediately practical character pressing themselves upon us at this very moment, and from which there is no escape. Is President Grant to succeed in his effort to abolish polygamy in Utah? Are we to fold our hands and tamely submit to the expulsion of the Bible from all our schools? Shall the oath be banished from our courts of justice? Shall we resist and antagonize in all lawful ways the open, determined and diabolical effort now made to destroy every Christian element which yet remains in our Government, and by constitutional enactments secure them to us and our posterity forever, while we lay the foundation for still further progress in the same direction?

Of all questions these are the most practical, as they are the ones which press themselves with the greatest urgency upon our immediate consideration. That we shall succeed in carrying this amendment, does not admit of doubt. The ablest thinkers of the nation are with us. As a question of talent, the weight is upon our side. The great majority of the best people of the nation are with us. They only need to be awakened to the importance of the issues which are made, and they will rise as the waves of the ocean when the storm descends upon it, and whelm beneath the tide of Christian sentiment, the audacious demands of an impious and alien atheism. This place calls up strange recollections. I have stood on this platform when this hall was filled with a raging, howling, blaspheming, pro-slavery mob, whose violence it took one hundred policemen, with the Chief of the Police at their head, to restrain; and in less than two years the streets of this city echoed to the strains of splendid regiments armed against slavery, kindled to the white heat of a burning patriotism, as they sang—

> "John Brown's body lies a mouldering in the grave;
> His soul is marching on."

God is with us; it is His prerogative to work with many or with few. It is not for us to know the times or the seasons which the Father hath put in His own power. We will succeed, whether in the near or the distant future. The mouth of the Lord hath spoken it. The kingdoms of this world shall become the kingdoms of our Lord and of his Christ.

The Rev. Dr. A. M. Milligan, of Pittsburg, was introduced by the President, and spoke as follows:

ADDRESS OF DR. A. M. MILLIGAN.

Mr. President: Our attention has been called to a *defect* of the Constitution—its *omission* of any express recognition of the authority of God over the nation. Such an omission is certainly a very serious defect in an instrument which proposes to define the relations of the Government to all parties to which it stands related; a defect which all sensible men, who seek to have their government enjoy amicable relations to the Supreme Ruler of the universe, would desire to have speedily remedied. Still, such omission may easily seem to have been an oversight—a thing taken for granted, or so well understood, that it needed no expression in that instrument; that it even now does not need to be inserted, being universally accepted. Hence, what need of this agitation? what need of another amendment?

Permit me, Mr. President, to call attention to something more than a mere defect, or failure to express in the Constitution a recognition of the divine authority over the nation. There is a virtual denial—a principle taught which is at variance with the doctrine of the divine authority over the nation. There are two opposite theories as to the source or origin of authority and power in government. The first is, that God is its author; that the power to set up and administer government is from Him ; that the revealed will of God is the rule by which this divine ordinance should be constituted; that the magistrate is the minister of God; and that to resist government so constituted and administered is to resist God and incur His wrath. This is the Christian theory, the teaching of the Bible, and accepted by the greatest statesmen and teachers of political science in ancient and modern times.

The other theory was first proclaimed by Hobbes, the celebrated English infidel, accepted by the infidel school of France, and taught in the French Encyclopædia. It proclaims that government is a mere human institution—a social compact—deriving all its authority from the consent of the governed, and having no higher law than the will of the people constitutionally expressed; that the magistrate is the mere servant of the people, having no higher obligation than to fulfill the will of his constituents, and responsible only to them.

This is designated the infidel theory. The one of these is the principle lying at the foundation of a Christian state, the other of an infidel state. This latter theory was boldly enunciated by the French National Assembly, when, at the close of the last century, they set up an infidel republic, emblazoning on their banner the motto "*There is no God*," and investing with divine honors "REASON" as their goddess.

This same theory of government is obscurely, but really and effectively, taught in our national Constitution. True, that instrument does not declare "*There is no God*," nor does it declare that human governments are not under divine authority. Such declarations would never have been accepted by the Christian people of this nation. Had such declarations appeared in that instrument, they would have raised such a storm as would have swept out of political existence the men who had offered the insult to our Christianity, and their names would have gone down with that of Thomas Paine to perpetual infamy. No ; the infidel element which participated in the framing of that instrument had not the courage to hazard such an experiment.

Come with me to the Constitution, and let us see what it teaches on this question. The first declaration referring to this is in the preamble: "We, the people of the United States," * * * "do ordain and establish this CONSTITUTION." There is here no allusion to any authority above "the people," under whose auspices, by whose permission, for whose glory, or in whatever relation to whom "*We, the people*," set up, in God's great empire, the Government of the United States. The inference plainly is, that the people create the government of themselves and for themselves, with no relations to any higher power. What would the Government of the United States think if a community of people were to set up a government in one of our territories without ever saying, "By your leave?"

One sentence recognizing the Divine authority would free the preamble from this charge; as it is, it may fairly be taken as the expression of the "social compact," or infidel theory of government, and, as a matter of fact, it is by multitudes of Christian people, as well as infidels, construed to mean nothing else.

Add to this the declaration of the Sixth Article, that "this Constitution and the laws made in pursuance thereof, shall be the *supreme law* of the land," and that "all executive and judicial officers, both of the United States and of the several States, shall be bound by oath or affirmation to support this Constitution; but no *religious test* shall ever be required as a qualification for any office;" and what have we? A Constitution ordained by the people without any acknowledgment of the authority of the Almighty; and then, lest some one should plead that still it is to be *understood* that God is over all, it is added: No *religious* test shall ever be required; not sectarian, denominational, or ecclesiastical test, but *religious* test. What does this mean? What is the meaning of *religion?* Webster's first definition is, "The recognition of God as an object of worship, love and *obedience.*" Let us apply this. No recognition of God as an object of obedience shall be required as a qualification for office, but only an oath to support this Constitution—the expressed will of the people. Add to all this, the fact that the name of God and all reference to His judgment is left out of the oath provided in the Constitution for the President, and administered to all officers, State and national, and we have in the Constitution a complete illustration of the theory of "No God in Government." As I have already stated, this is not openly expressed, but covertly disguised under the flattering idea that all power is in the hands of the people.

Now, the question recurs, granting that this is so: What importance attaches to it? What harm can come from it? To this, I reply:

First.—It places the nation in the attitude of professing a principle that is at variance with the truth, and with the sentiment of the nation. Is that a desirable position in which to stand before the world, proclaiming a falsehood which we know and believe to be such?

Mr. President, this nation believes there is a God, and that He is the Supreme Ruler of nations. The nation has proclaimed this in her Declaration of Independence, Articles of Confederation, and in her State Constitutions, and in a thousand other ways; and yet in our Constitution we turn our back upon our history, and by our criminal silence give the lie to all our other professions. Is not this a humiliating attitude for a great Christian nation to occupy? Shall we occupy this position because an infinitesimal minority of the people demand it? Shall the Constitution of the nation express the truth believed by the great Christian majority of the nation, or shall it endorse a falsehood proposed by a handful of infidels in it?

Second.—The Constitution is a great educator. Regarded as expressing the combined wisdom of the nation, it is looked up to as authority. Our ideas of right and wrong are largely derived from law. Whatever is law we are inclined to regard as right. The Constitution is the *supreme* law of the land, towering above State laws and constitutions and acts of Congress. It is the test to which all laws must be brought. It is the highest and most authoritative legal teacher in the land. Now, if this instrument teaches that no obedience or subjection is due from the nation or its rulers to God—that the magistrate, as such, is under no obligation to God, and owes no obedience to his law—what must be the consequence? Take away the fear of God, and where will be our honesty, fidelity, incorruptibility? What restraint is left that cannot easily be evaded? What security has society against the most wholesale robbery, bribery, and every other malfeasance in office? The theory that "politics has nothing to do with religion," is but the echo of the Constitution, and it lies at the bottom of all the corruption that has entered into our political system.

Men who do not believe the theory will practice according to it so long as it is constitutional and suits their purposes. If, then, we do not wish to educate and raise up a nation of political infidels and atheists, let us amend our text-book, and teach through our Constitution that the nation and its rulers are amenable to God and His law, and let the national conscience be educated in the true principles of national prosperity and security.

Third.—It exerts a malign influence upon other nations. The nations of the Old World are struggling up toward republican liberty. They look to this nation as their model and guide. And when they study our institutions to ascertain the secret of our prosperity, they go to our Constitution, and the result is that the Commune of Paris, the Turners of Germany, and the Internationals of Europe, point to us as an infidel nation, prove their assertion by the Constitution, and attribute our liberty and prosperity to our infidelity. What a dangerous mistake! Like a false signal on a stormy, rock-reefed sea! How many nations may make shipwreck, and attribute their ruin to the false light hung out at our mast-head? No one who knows our history, and the secret of our prosperity, can doubt that the mightiest force in our nation, and that which has conduced most to our success, is our Christianity. Take that away, and you leave Hamlet out of the play. Let us tell the struggling nations, when they ask for the way that led us to our present proud position, that it was the covenant made with God in the cabin of the Mayflower, and our fathers' faith in God, that led us hither.

The *Fourth* evil arising from the present attitude of the Constitution is that it leaves us no legal basis for the Christian features of our Government.

As I have already remarked, Christianity forms an essential element of our nationality, and enters into all the features of our governmental character. Our Christian Sabbath; our chaplains in Congress, army, prisons, etc.; our Bible in the schools; our marriage laws; our fasts and thanksgivings; our judicial oath; our system of morality, are all distinctively Christian. These have grown up with us, and are a part of our national life. But there is no authority for them in the Constitution; on the other hand, they are contrary to the very theory of government of which that instrument is the exponent—the theory which forbids the nation, as such, to have to do with religion. Is it not having to do with religion to place legal restraints upon the desecration of the Christian Sabbath; to teach the Christian's Bible to the nation's children in the public schools; to appoint Christian ministers to preach the gospel to the National Congress, to the army and navy? Is it not having to do with religion to require the magistrate and the witness to qualify by an oath taken in the name of the Christian's God, or on the Gospels; or to call the nation to worship God in exercises of prayer and thanksgiving? Is it not restraining the free exercise of his religion to prevent the Mormon's enjoyment of his polygamy, or arrest him in the administration of the highest censure of his church—the "Blood Atonement"—by the Danite's dagger? In all these, and many other respects, the conduct of the nation is inconsistent with the spirit and letter of its Constitution. This may have been a matter of comparatively little consequence, as long as all were agreed, and there was none to call in question these acts or their constitutionality; but now that an earnest and able body of men have united and organized themselves, with the declared purpose of sweeping every trace of Christianity from our national life—it becomes a matter of the highest consequence on which side of this great controversy the Constitution stands;

and if it be against us, we are left the alternative either to give up our Christianity or amend our Constitution.

My *Fifth* and last reason for seeking a change of the Constitution in this particular, is that as it is, it is a standing insult offered by the nation to its God—the author of its existence and prosperity. We have virtually said in that instrument which is the highest expression of the nation's will : "*Our lips are our own : who is Lord over us?*"

Why has not God smitten us as he did infidel France? There is but one reason ; the insult was not understood, nor intended by the nation. The attention of the nation has never until recently been called to the matter, and even yet many Christian men will hardly consent to such an interpretation. But now the question is forced to an issue, and we must settle it—we can no longer occupy an attitude of neutrality or inaction. Like Pontius Pilate we have a person on our hands, and like him we may ask, "What shall I do with Jesus who is called Christ?" We must either crucify or crown him ; and like the Jewish nation our decision will seal our future destiny. Either like them we will reject him and perish, or, becoming a kingdom of our Lord and His Christ, we shall fill the earth and endure forever.

During our recent struggle to save the nation's life from the assault of a terrible rebellion, the Senate of the United States requested President Lincoln to call the nation to fasting, humiliation and prayer, that "God for Christ's sake would save the nation." That prayer was heard and answered, and the nation saved ; and ever since we have had our yearly thanksgiving at the call of the President to render thanks to God for the mercies of the year. Is this consistent ? Shall we ask national favors from One whose being or authority we are unwilling to recognize in the National Constitution? Jefferson refused to proclaim a fast in time of trial on this very ground, and said : "I believe the Government of the United States is interdicted by the Constitution from interfering with religious institutions." What claim have we on Christ to save or bless us, unless we recognize His authority over us? Protection and allegiance are correlates, and we cannot claim the one unless we render the other. On the other hand, subjects refusing allegiance expose themselves to the wrath of their Sovereign.

And now the infidel junto have proclaimed their determination that all these national acts of religion shall cease, and they make their demand on constitutional grounds. Their position is consistent, and we are left the alternative either to conform our Constitution to our practice or lapse into atheism. The issue is fairly joined; the lines are clearly drawn, and the respective parties are ranging themselves under their respective banners. The demands of liberalism "that all laws looking to the enforcement of Christian morality shall be abrogated," and every vestige of Christianity swept out of the Government, present one side of the question. Our Amendment is the other. When this contest is over, there will be no longer room for the plea of ignorance or forgetfulness on the part of the people; there will be no indefiniteness in the letter of the Constitution. The nation will stand squarely on the one side or the other—either Christian in Constitution as well as character, or infidel in character as well as Constitution. Our relations to the Kingdom of Christ will be well defined, and we will as a nation either crown or crucify him. Viewed in this light the issue is momentous. The hour is freighted with destiny. This great nation, standing on an elevated platform in the presence of the civilized world, is about to recognize its King and crown him, or to renounce all allegiance and crucify him.

The Committee on Permanent Organization reported the following officers of the National Association for the coming year, who were elected amid loud applause:

PRESIDENT:

The HON. FELIX R. BRUNOT.

VICE-PRESIDENTS:

His Excellency, JAMES M. HARVEY, *Governor of Kansas.*
The Hon. J. W. McCLURG, *Ex-Governor of Missouri.*
The Hon. W. H. CUMBACK, *Lieutenant-Governor of Indiana.*
The Hon. LORENZO SAWYER, *U. S. Circuit Court, San Francisco, Cal.*
The Hon. G. W. BROOKS, *U. S. District Court, North Carolina.*
The Hon. M. B. HAGANS, *Superior Court of Cincinnati.*
The Hon. J. ROCKWELL, *Superior Court of Massachusetts.*
The Hon. ELLIS A. APGAR, *State Sup't of Public Instruction, N. J.*
The Hon. DANIEL B. BRIGGS, *State Sup't of Public Instruction, Mich.*
The Hon. ALONZO ABERNETHY, *State Sup't of Public Instruction, Iowa.*
The Hon. A. N. FISHER, *State Sup't of Public Instruction, Nevada.*
The Hon. JOSIAH H. DRUMMOND, LL. D., *Portland, Maine.*
JOHN ALEXANDER, Esq., *Philadelphia, Pa.*
CHARLES G. NAZRO, Esq., *Boston, Mass.*
The Hon. THOMAS W. BICKNELL, *Commissioner of Public Schools, R. I.*
JAMES W. TAYLOR, Esq., *Newburg, N. Y.*
Prof. TAYLER LEWIS, LL.D., *Union College, N. Y.*
The Right Rev. JOHN B. KERFOOT, D.D., *Bishop Prot. Ep. Church, Diocese of Pittsburg.*
The Rev. T. L. CUYLER, D.D., *Brooklyn, N. Y.*
The Rev. LEVI SCOTT, D.D., *Bishop of the M. E. Church, Delaware.*
Prof. JULIUS H. SEELYE, D.D., *Amherst College, Mass.*
The Right Rev. F. D. HUNTINGTON, D.D., *Bishop of the Prot. Ep. Church, Diocese of Central New York.*
The Right Rev. C. P. McILVANE, D.D., LL.D., D.C.L., *Bishop of the Prot. Ep. Church, Diocese of Ohio.*
The Rev. A. A. MINER, D.D., *President of Tuft's College, Mass.*
The Rev. JONATHAN EDWARDS, D.D., *Peoria, Ill.*
The Rev. EDMUND S. JANES, D.D., *Bishop of the M. E. Church, New York.*
The Rev. HENRY J. FOX, D.D., *Charleston, S. C.*
The Right Rev. W. M. GREEN, D.D., *Bishop of the Prot. Ep. Church, Diocese of Mississippi.*
Vice-Chancellor J. GORGAS, *University of the South, Tenn.*
President WILLIAM CAREY CRANE, D.D., *Baylor University, Texas.*
The Right Rev. G. T. BEDELL, D.D., *Assist. Bishop of Prot. Ep. Church, Ohio.*
The Right Rev. G. D. CUMMINS, D.D., *Assist. Bishop of the Prot. Ep. Church, Diocese of Kentucky.*

The Rev. C. S. FINNEY, D.D., *Formerly President of Oberlin College, Oberlin, Ohio.*
The Rev. T. A. MORRIS, D.D., *Bishop of the M. E. Church, Springfield, O.*
The Rev. J. H. McILVAINE, D.D., *Newark, N. J.*
The Rev. M. SIMPSON, D.D., *Bishop of the M. E. Church, Pa.*
The Rev. J. BLANCHARD, D.D., *President of Wheaton College, Ill.*
Prof. O. N. STODDARD, LL.D., *Wooster University, Ohio.*
Prof. J. R. W. SLOANE, D.D., *Ref. Presb. Theo. Seminary, Allegheny, Pa.*
The Rev. E. R. CRAVEN, D.D., *Newark, N. J.*
The Rev. JOS. CUMMINGS, D.D., LL.D., *President of the Wesleyan University, Middletown, Conn.*
The Rev. STEPHEN H. TYNG, D.D., *New York.*
The Rev. F. MERRICK, D.D., LL.D., *President of the Ohio University, Delaware, Ohio.*
The Rev. A. D. MAYO, D.D., *Springfield, Mass.*
The Rev. JOHN B. DALES, D.D., *Philadelphia, Pa.*
The Rev. JOSEPH T. COOPER, D.D., *Pittsburg, Pa.*
The Rev. Dr. J. BANVARD, *Paterson, N. J.*
The Rev. C. H. EDGAR, D.D., *Easton, Pa.*
The Rev. WILLIAM NAST, D.D., *Editor of German Publications of the M. E. Church, Cincinnati, Ohio.*
The Rev. JOHN S. STONE, D.D., *Epis. Theo. School, Cambridge, Mass.*
The Rev. H. DYER, D.D., *Corresponding Sec. of Evang. Knowl. Society, N. Y.*
The Rev. THOMAS SPROULL, D.D., *Ref. Presb. Theo. Seminary, Allegheny, Pa.*
President W. F. KING, D.D., *Cornell College, Iowa.*
President JAMES W. STRONG, D.D., *Carleton College, Minn.*
President THOMAS HOLMES, D.D., *Union Christian College, Ind.*

GENERAL SECRETARY:

The Rev. D. McALLISTER, 410 *West Forty-third Street, New York.*

CORRESPONDING SECRETARY:

The Rev. T. P. STEVENSON, 38 *North Sixteenth Street, Philadelphia.*

RECORDING SECRETARY:

The Rev. W. W. BARR, *Philadelphia.*

TREASURER:

SAMUEL AGNEW, Esq., 1126 *Arch Street, Philadelphia.*

EXECUTIVE COMMITTEE:

The Secretaries and Treasurer of the Association, *ex-officio.*

R. B. STERLING, ... *Philadelphia, Pa.*
JOSHUA COWPLAND, ... "
JOHN ALEXANDER, ... "
JAS. S. MARTIN, ... "
The Rev. S. O. WYLIE, D.D., ... "
ROBERT TAYLOR, ... "
WM. McKNIGHT, ... "
THOS. WALKER, ... "
THOS. BROWN, ... "

Henry Harrison,	*New York.*
Robert B. Maxwell,	"
William Neely,	"
Walter T. Miller,	"
Jas. Wiggins,	"
Henry O'Neill,	"
Geo. Silver,	"
James Spence,	"
Hugh Carlisle,	"
The Rev. Wm. S. Owens,	*Indiana, Pa.*
D. Chesnut,	*Pittsburg.*
Henry Martin,	*Cincinnati.*

The name of the President nominated was greeted with hearty cheers, and the vote being taken by the Chairman of the Committee, Mr. Brunot was unanimously elected. After the applause had subsided, the President-elect arose and spoke as follows:

When called upon to perform any labor or stand in any position, and the call came to him to do his duty as a Christian, he had never answered "No." When requested to serve as presiding officer of this Convention, he had urged that some one better fitted for the position might be chosen in his place. But it had been judged best for him to occupy the chair, and he had consented so to do. And now, upon his election to the presidency of the National Association, he felt like yielding to some other one, better qualified to stand at the head of this movement. But when made the choice of this Convention, he would not hold back. He was proud to stand in this relation to this movement. Though somewhat advanced in years, he expected to live to see our cause triumph. God never puts a truth into the hearts of men without giving also the power which will sooner or later make that truth victorious. In conclusion, he thanked the Convention for their very kind toleration of the manner in which he had presided over its deliberations.

The Convention then adjourned *sine die*, with prayer and the benediction by the Rev. E. B. Miner, D. D., of New York.

www.ingramcontent.com/pod-product-compliance
Lightning Source LLC
LaVergne TN
LVHW011120110826
845150LV00008B/2200

* 9 7 8 1 4 2 5 5 0 4 9 9 1 *